Lash MASTERS

By Chrysalis House Publishing

Lash Masters - Copyright © 2014 by Chrysalis House Publishing

ISBN 9781495316210

All rights reserved. No part of this publication may be reproduced, distributed, or transmitted in any form or by any means, including photocopying, recording, or other electronic or mechanical methods, without the prior written permission of the publisher, except in the case of brief quotations embodied in articles and certain other non commercial uses permitted by copyright law. For permission requests, write to the publisher, addressed: "Attention: Permissions Coordinator," at the address below.

Chrysalis House Publishing
Louise Prunty
Lower Ground
7 Newton Place
Glasgow
G3 7PR
United Kingdom

publishinguk@me.com
www.chrysalishousepublishing.com

Contents

Foreword...4

Chapter 1: Karen Betts & Bridgette Softley.............................7

Chapter 2: Louise Prunty...13

Chapter 3: Nadia Afanaseva..21

Chapter 4: Julia (Yulia) Iskusnykh...27

Chapter 5: Stefani Altieri...33

Chapter 6: Britta Krueger..49

Chapter 7: Kathryn Popplestone..57

Chapter 8: Suzette Zuena..65

Chapter 9: Leah Lynch...75

Chapter 10: Francesca Middleton..83

Chapter 11: Zola Nemorin...91

Chapter 12: Loreta Jasilionyte...101

Chapter 13: Lindsay Carey..109

Chapter 14: Marisol Price..115

Chapter 15: Ria (Sotiria) Hountas..119

Foreword

Joy
WATSON-CARR

The timing could not be more perfect for this book – the eyelash revolution is upon us! From an odd little specialist treatment, to mainstream salon, to the new dawn of volume and advanced techniques – those crazy, infuriating little lashes have refused to go away and have instead carved out a whole new mini-industry for themselves!

When asked to edit this book I jumped at the chance; I couldn't wait to hear what the real masters, the pioneers if you like, had to say. If I'm honest however, I really wasn't sure what to expect. What I went on to read, both surprised and delighted me. Of course there were different viewpoints, different starting points, different life experiences, even different cultures, languages and countries all coming together; but what excited me the most was that; sweeping all this diversity aside, the fundamental philosophies and beliefs of every single artist featured, were near identical.

Learn Well
Work Hard
Practice
Never Give Up

If I had to sum up the book in just a handful of words, those would be them. Great things come to those who put a pair of tweezers in each hand and no matter what, refuse to put them down again…

It has been a pleasure to read such interesting and inspirational stories, I hope you enjoy the book, and I wish you every success in your ongoing lash journey.

Chapter 1

Karen BETTS

Bridgette SOFTLEY

You're good ... but are you a Master?

Nouveau Lashes are the lash innovators. Our experts have been leading the lash industry and setting training standards since 2005. We are committed to the personal development of each of our students and believe achieving flawless eyelash extensions is down to a lot more than just high quality products. At Nouveau, high quality products are a given, synonymous with the brands existing reputation in other sectors such as permanent cosmetics; this is why we are able to concentrate on what's important – helping you achieve your full lash potential.

Softley quotes "Knowing enough is never enough, which is why we place a strong emphasis on promoting the need for the correct training. The ability to adapt the treatment using the right techniques for each client is fundamental to the end result and the ultimate difference between a lash technician and a lash master. In order to really shine, professionals need to push themselves ... to strive for perfection, to keep learning new skills and to become even better at the skills they already have".

Betts explains "Bridgette and I went on to develop Nouveau Lashes, whilst looking for a way to help clients who had lost their natural lashes through chemotherapy or alopecia. Disappointed with what we found in the UK, we attended Cosmoprof in Hong Kong (the worldwide leading event for the professional beauty sector) and it was there we came across a demonstration of something that looked like spiders legs being applied to a ladies own eyelashes! Having studied the current techniques, Bridgette and I could not contain our excitement on our return journey to the UK, at the potential of this concept. We immediately began working on our own eyelash extension system, subsequently putting together a training programme which is now considered to be the original and best in the industry. This has been echoed by our recent nomination for Best Lash Supplier of 2014 by The Guild Award of Excellence".

Just a quick flick through the glossies will tell every fashionista exactly what she needs to know – from the red carpet to the stage, from the video promo to the charity appearance, celebrities everywhere are falling for Nouveau Lashes. In the early days, before long lush lashes became the new mani/pedi and the multi million pound industry it is today, we have one very influential lady to thank for this. Avid hair extension fan and the most photographed woman of the time - Victoria Beckham, visited her personal beautician who had recently qualified in Nouveau Lashes and advised Victoria that semi permanent eyelash extensions from Nouveau Lashes were the next big thing. Always the trend setter Victoria became one of the first celebrities to showcase our alluring yet natural lashes.

There was a media frenzy and before we knew it we had gone from delivering 10 training classes a month to 9 classes a week. That little pot of unglamorous looking spider's legs was now an ambitious plan to create a brand new beauty service focused solely on the eyes, one with great results for the client and impressive retail figures for the salon or therapist.

4 years on and with 3 very distinct target markets for the brand – the glamorous, work hard play harder 20 something, the 35 plus professional who wants to look her best at work, and the yummy mummy, as well as a number of other brands entering the market place, we held a focus group to discuss how Nouveau Lashes would stay ahead in the industry. It was at this time we were approached by the beauty buyer of London's most prestigious store - Harrods. The upmarket department store wanted to offer eyelash treatments but they wanted a service that catered for the time-poor, yet demanding lady. After a number of focus groups and market research it became apparent we needed to develop 2 more lash treatments - one based on fast beauty and one that actually involved no extensions but enhanced the client's natural lashes in a sophisticated and understated way.

Today you will recognise those developments as Let's Go

Lashes, the express eyelash system which thickens lashes but in a fraction of the time traditional lash treatments take, and LVL. Loved by celebrity make-up artist Lisa Eldridge, LVL stands for Length, Volume and Lift. A treatment for the natural lash that doesn't involve extensions and lasts up to six weeks.

Following popular demand Nouveau Lashes also supply an extensive strip lash range and have worked with reality TV stars such as Amy Childs, Millie Mackintosh and make-up artist Gary Cockerill to help them develop their own range of strip lashes. Millie Mackintosh for Nouveau Lashes is available in high street store Selfridges of London and from online retailers Amazon. Most recently Nouveau Lashes developed Ultrabond Strip with the World's leading experts in developing medical grade adhesives. This collaboration has spawned a new and superior strip lash adhesive; that has amazing bonding strength as well as being latex free, heat and humidity resistant and suitable for use on natural and synthetic strip lashes applied by experienced eyelash professionals and the public alike.

Softley and Betts explain that whilst their personal goal still remains to find a suitable product for clients who lose their natural lashes as a result of accident or illness, the lash effect has never been more now. Every day it becomes a part of the daily beauty routine of more image conscious women all over the UK... and beyond. With 5133 trained Nouveau Lashes technicians and 23 international distributors Nouveau Lashes is determined to remain at the forefront of the industry.

LASH MASTERS

Recently tasking Propaganda - the marketing agency famous for making brands such as ghd and Illamasqua household names - with helping develop our strategy for future growth, we are eagerly awaiting their brand discovery feedback … watch this space.

Existing and new customers can be assured that when they train with Nouveau Lashes they will be more than just a lash technician … they will have the foundation to become a lash master and are guaranteed eyelash fluttering success.

Company Details
Tel: 0844 801 6828
Twitter: @NouveauLashes
Website: www.nouveaulashes.co.uk
Winner of Best Lash Supplier 2014 - Guild Awards of Excellence

Chapter 2

Louise **PRUNTY**

With a BSc in Instrumentation with Applied Physics and an MSc in Ecommerce, the industry I found myself in was quite different to where I had imagined myself. Three years after I graduated from university I realised was dissatisfied with my working environment, and, after receiving a holistic therapy treatment, decided to change career. I re-trained and started a self-employed business in the professional beauty and holistic therapy sector.

My first business was called Louise's Therapy. I ran this on a part time basis whilst having a full time job until I had built up my clientele; once I thought I had enough, I made the jump. I had never been so scared. It didn't take long for me to step into trainer mode with clients, they learned lots about the treatments they were getting and clients kept asking if I offered training courses. Due to my training background I thought this seemed like a good idea. So later that year I moved into larger premises, hired someone to help with training and developed several different accredited training courses. The business was re-branded Caledonian Therapy

Academy and became a limited company. At this point we had only been offering holistic treatments and training, but after a mentoring session with my friend Monette, I decided to expand into beauty training. The company progressed from there and I fell into product development. I wanted to produce a better glue than was on the market at the time, the eyelash extension glue we purchased from our local trade store was highly fumed, had a 3 month shelf life and more often that not when we had purchased kits the glue had completely dried out. So out of need for a longer lasting and better glue, the 'Glam Lash' flexi glue was born. After this I produced the world's first pre-blended semi permanent mascara 'Myscara' and several other beauty products. There have been ups and downs along the way and we have had our share of challenges; mainly staff issues and money issues that come with a rapidly expanding company. However it has been an amazing adventure building a business from nothing into something so successful.

In 2012 I set up a new business with a very successful business person. This meant I had investment funds and resources to grow the business far more quickly than I would be able to do alone. Assets from my old business were transferred to the new business and I begin my new chapter in this corporate business. I learned many things during this period, the main thing I found frustrating however was how slow corporate organisations work. I felt as if my wings had been clipped. It's just the way things are in that type of business, but as an entrepreneur it was difficult. An opportunity arose to exit this business and I took it … unsure what I would be doing next, but confident something would develop. On my last day at HQ I had a marketing meeting, and was asked about placing adverts in the 'Eyelash magazine'. "There is no such magazine on the European market aimed at beauty therapists" I said, and her response was "oh really"?!

Due to the experience I have had in writing beauty books, a magazine had entered my mind previously. It was in my 'little black book' of ideas, but had been shelved for several years as I hadn't the time, motivation or confidence to try and pull it off.

However now, it all seemed to make perfect sense and I knew I could do it. I had intended that by the end of that day I would have a business idea and this was it. I had a four hour train journey home after the meeting and I wasted no time. I decided on a name, purchased a domain name, set up a Facebook business page and opened a bank account online. Lash Inc Magazine was born!

At the time of writing I am working on issue 3 of Lash Inc. The magazine is currently published quarterly and doing great. I get such a feeling of satisfaction seeing the magazine when it's finished and have made some wonderful friends and business contacts through producing the magazine. I have big plans for the magazine and already we have launched 'The Lash Box' - A box of samples that brings fantastic products from manufacturers and distributors directly to the lash artist. The other product I have been working on is this book. Lash Masters is another idea which popped into my head during a marketing course I had attended. At this moment it is available to pre-order on Amazon and we have already sold 100's and ranked 10.978 out of over 15 Million books, I am hoping for a number 1 in its category. I hope you enjoy reading the stories in this book as much as we have during the production and you can find some inspiration from them.

I decided that publishing would be the main focus for now as this has the most potential to bring in money, and I also wanted to re-kindle a business I had started which hadn't really got going with, Chrysalis House Publishing. I had used the name to publish a book on Speed Writing which I had written and planned to seek out great authors and publish their books. I hadn't had the time to spend on this until now, but now everything was shiny and new again and I felt inspired.

I hope to inspire others through sharing my story of how I doubled my income and changed my life significantly by being inspired and from just one book.

As I said, I developed professional beauty products (mainly in the eye treatment category). I needed a manual to cover a new type of treatment I had developed. So out of need, I wrote one from scratch. After writing it I thought I would find out how to list it on Amazon. I thought I would make a small amount of income from the sales and would have been quite happy with that. However I actually managed to double my income instead. I didn't realise that the book would make me an authority in my niche and distributors came knocking at my door. I spent no money on advertising and was struggling to keep up with demand for our products. Having a book in my opinion is the best form of advertising there is.

I also gained interest from investors and was invited on to the premier episode of 'The Angel' on Sky 1 with Billionaire John Caudwell. I had discovered the secret of growing my business and now I get to share everything I have learned with others and help others grow their businesses through publishing a book.

I usually become inspired in one of two ways:
1) Having a challenge to overcome or having something that I absolutely have to do with no way (yet) of doing it. For some people this is counterproductive, they worry, they get brain fog and panic. For me it brings clarity and my mind goes into overdrive thinking of new ideas to solve it.

2) Listening to others, especially training courses. I usually get at the very least one massive idea from conferences and training courses I attend. When you are all out of ideas and inspiration of your own you have to seek out external inspiration. Think of it as 'Your Box'. Your box is filled with all the stuff you know, you have probably tried everything in it in every combination. When what's inside your box doesn't work then you have to dip into the knowledge, inspiration and tools in someone else's box. As everyone's learning and experiences are different, everyone's box is different so there is a wealth of knowledge and inspiration out there.

When I have that initial idea, Google is my go-to place. I need to do research to find out as much as possible and to feed my creativity with every bit of information I can find. I have learned so many things about marketing, but for me the biggest idea was the concept of focusing of niche markets. Niche markets don't have the massive numbers of customers but I believe they are the most lucrative.

Inspiration is every part of my business, I am constantly being inspired to improve, to create new products offer new services, to inspire others. Without inspiration there is no business.

I was inspired recently by a rainbow! From this I developed the Spectrum Strategy (R). I am currently writing a book on this. I believe there are 7 key parts to running a successful, profitable business. It's called the spectrum strategy (R) as each part is named from the colours of the light spectrum:

R is for (Red) Resources
O is for (Orange) Opportunity
Y is for (Yellow) You

G is for (Green) Gift
B is for (Blue) Book
I is for (Indigo) Innovation
V is for (Violet) Vision
Let's take Opportunity as an example:

"If opportunity doesn't knock, build a door." Milton Berle

is one of my favourite quotes. I know so many people who say, "No one gives me an opportunity", "All the opportunities have been taken" and variations on this.

I will give you an example of 'building a door', I had been on a training course where one of the speakers was a dummies author. I estimated that the chances of someone giving me the opportunity of writing a Dummies ® book was pretty slim. The speaker actually said "There is not point in contacting them, everything is in house now and they do not take anyone on." I love a good challenge. What did I do? I built my door! I contacted several departments in Dummies ® until I eventually got the correct one, many emails took place until I was given a number to call and now I have the opportunity to write a Dummies book ®. If you want to do something, find a way to make it happen. Anything is possible.

Everyone, no matter what their qualifications, experience, or writing skills can write a good book. I want to share my knowledge to everyone who wants to learn. So many people read books but only a small fraction write books. I want to help business owners have the best marketing tool they can.

Once you take action everything else will be much easier.
If you take action you have done the hardest part.
When writing a book to promote your business many people find it difficult to narrow down what to write about. If you email me with a link to your website and I will do at least an hours' worth of research (for free) to find out the best type of book you could write to promote yourself or your business.

Take Action! Email me with your business website address and let me know the unique selling point of your product or service.

I will email you back with my free suggestions and plan on how to write your book and get it to market. If you are looking to have your article published in Lash Inc magazine please also get in touch, we are always looking for fresh content.

Louise Prunty
Helping others publish and profit!

www.lashinc.eu
www.chrysalishousepublishing.com
www.louiseprunty.com
louiseprunty@me.com
Tel: +447828811190 / +441413328814

Chapter 3

Nadia AFANASEVA

Before doing eyelash extensions I was a university student. I was studying in St. Petersburg, Russia. St. Petersburg is the cultural centre and cultural capital of Russia. There is a huge amount of cultural heritage in our city, there are always plenty of fascinating exhibitions and events going on, and always something interesting for students to do.

When I was a student I worked part-time in a cosmetics company and learned specialist techniques with make-up. Like any girl I liked to look good and always tried to follow the trends. At that time eyelash extensions were just beginning to be developed. My first acquaintance with lash extensions was as a client. I really liked the idea of not having to spend much time on make-up, and loved the way my eyes became so expressive, I thought it would be great to offer this service to my clients.

As a child I was very fond of drawing and enjoyed doing fine, creative work like embroidery and knitting, so I was sure that doing eyelash extensions would be very easy for me.

At that time there were not too many schools around teaching eyelash extensions, there were mainly just practicing stylists. I took a course from my own lash stylist but there wasn't too much information given, we were just told about the tools and equipment needed, and were shown how to attach an eyelash. The class was held within one day in a small stuffy little room, packed to capacity, table to table. Four of us were practicing on the same model, and I felt I really didn't get enough practice that day. So that's how I got my first certificate as a lash stylist.

My first model was my sister, she's a little younger than me, so was quite obedient at lying still on the couch during my long hours of training. Then I tested my lashes on all my girlfriends, and since there were many of them I began to see immediate results. I felt no discomfort or fatigue when working, and noticed that every time I was getting better and better results, and that's how I came to realize how much I loved doing eyelash extensions.

I was so happy that I found myself in life.

The most important thing for me is the joy of a customer after their treatment. I am a perfectionist and a workaholic by nature so I can happily work 12-15 hours a day. I rarely take days off. Added to this is my sincere love of my job that makes me think of eyelashes constantly, and pushes me to keep on progressing. That's how new ideas are born and old methods are improved.

I always take pictures of my work, I sometimes record my seminars for further analysis and correcting mistakes. I am very critical towards my work and make every effort to gain the most customer satisfaction. I'm constantly trying new materials and techniques and follow all the new innovations the industry.

Eyelash extensions is a whole industry in itself, there are many stylists who carry out eyelash treatments. Some people are working purely in order to earn money so their main concerns are less cost and more tips. There are others however who truly love their job and constantly improve their skills. These therapists get so much more than just money from their clients – they get their clients' loyalty, and their gratitude for a high quality job.

An eyelash extension treatment is a certain art, it is something so much more than just attaching an extension to a natural lash. All clients are different and have eyes of a different size and shape, they have different eyelids and eyebrows, different lash growth, and different eye and skin colour. You need to style the whole look of the eye area, not just the lashes. Pick something individual and unique. Imagine how it will fit that particular client. It's not merely about giving a great set of eyelash extensions but about ensuring every aspect of their overall look is harmoniously combined. The greatest pleasure at the end of the procedure is when the client screams in joy in front of the mirror.

My husband and I moved to New York recently so I was faced with the challenge of upping sticks and relocating my salon. I now have a small and cozy studio in the heart of Manhattan on 7th Avenue between Times Square and Central Park. We are open 7 days a week, from 9 am to 11 pm. We teach classes on a regular basis, as well as working with clients.

At the time of this interview I run five different classes for different levels of experience. There are courses for beginners who are new in the eyelash extensions industry. There are courses for stylists who are already working but want to improve their skills and expand their knowledge. There are also courses for professionals who want to perfect their skills.

We use a large amount of video material, photo material and graphics on our classes, we give a tutorial and of course they practice their new acquired skills on models. Our classes teach you everything you need to get working, I offer only materials which I use and have tested personally.

We also conduct group trainings and retreats; at present only within the United States of America, but we are negotiating about opening schools in Europe, due to the high volume of European requests we receive.

I'm always happy to share my experience with anybody, no matter where they are located.

My main advice is to decide for yourself whether eyelash extensions is your cup of tea or not and to understand why you do it. When you live doing what you love, you feel neither time nor fatigue, you live from the energy of your discoveries and achievements.

Learn constantly, and take as many classes as possible, it will give you an understanding of the subject from different perspectives. Each stylist and teacher has his own thoughts, secrets and tricks.

The more you invest in your education, the more will come back to you. Very often my students buy DVD training or get Skype consultations before coming to my courses. I don't recommend this – nothing can replace live communication with a trainer.

When choosing a trainer also be warned, there are people teaching who have just finished their studies themselves; and who without any experience, only their initial training, have gone on to open a school or have begun to teach. There are also trainers who have been known to buy pictures from little-known stylists to advertise themselves. All these people with their non-professional approach only will cast a shadow of disappointment over this beautiful industry. Always choose a

LASH MASTERS

trainer by his or her large portfolio.

__Be attentive and truly love your job!__

http://eyelash-training.com

Chapter 4

Julia (Yulia) ISKUSNYKH

Hello readers - let's get acquainted - my name is Julia Iskusnykh. I am the founder, director and leading technician and instructor of "Julia Iskusnykh School-Studio". I'm also a practicing master lash artist with over 7 years' experience, a graduate of one of the best schools in Ukraine and Russia, a graduate of the Academy of Eyelash Extension of Dobronravova Olga (St. Petersburg), Academy of Look Design «Lash & Brow Design Academy» (Moscow), School of Eyelash Extension of Eva Bond, winner of the International Coach Certificate, Certificate of the First international conference Lashboom. I am also a certified coach of bio-curl for natural lashes and in the application of semi-permanent mascara. I was the Ukraine 2013 champion for Classic Eyelash Extensions, and the Ukraine 2012 champion for Eyelash Decoration and Image Creation. I have also won the Audience Award in the I-Ukrainian competition for Eyelash Extensions and am a judge of all Ukrainian lash competitions.

After graduating from school with honours, I had a choice of who to become. At that time banking and law were fashionable, but I wanted "to create". And there I made my first decision – to be a hairstylist. This was interesting, captivating, exciting, - and so began a career in the beauty industry. After the first contests came the first victories. And then, as a result of my work and achievements - an invitation to work in elite beauty salon. Work was buzzing, everything was going great. But the time always comes when you want to change something in life, to learn something new.

I was visiting the exhibition "Inter Sharm" in Kiev, when I came across a flyer: "Eyelash Extension Training" - an eyelash extension - that was the newest thing in the beauty industry. So on March 12, 2007 there was a significant event in my life – the first time I placed a pair of eyelash tweezers in my hands - it was like a first step for a child – a step into the future. And then, step by step, eyelash after eyelash ... I gained my first knowledge of this area in Kiev, in a company called «Prof Line», I was there at the very beginning of this new profession and was the first Master Lash Artist in my city.

I've always been fascinated by the different look and design we can give our eyes. Our eyes are the most powerful weapon of female seduction. A languid, soft, piercing glance that can instantly turn the head of even a stranger .... unprecedented self-confidence ... an exquisite and delicate charm - your eyes can do wonders not only with others, but first and foremost with your mood and self-awareness. How is that possible? Today, you can in just a couple hours you can really transform your look and make it magical, and all because of the unique techniques of eyelash extensions.

My lash school and studio is based in Lugansk City, Ukraine. For our dear clients in the studio-school we offer: individual eyelash extensions, volume extensions, lash decoration, lash bio-curling, semi-permanent mascara, eyebrow shaping, semi-permanent eyebrow restoration and 6D bio-tattooing of eyebrows. Education is another area of the studio-school. For learners we offer a variety of courses, designed both for beginners just discovering the world of eyelash extensions and for professionals who want to improve their skills or learn about the latest fashions in the field.

My lash school courses are unique; it is my vast experience and knowledge, gained from some of the best schools and courses in eyelash extensions, and from many years of experience in the field, that has enabled me to flourish within the beauty industry. As creative director, I was able to select the most valuable knowledge and techniques, and gather them together into a series of training packages, to help develop a new generation of professionals.

I was the Ukraine 2013 champion for Classic Eyelash Extensions, and the Ukraine 2012 champion for Eyelash Decoration and Image Creation. I have also won the Audience Award in the I-Ukrainian competition for Eyelash Extensions and am a judge of all Ukrainian lash competitions.

I would advise beginners in the industry to always choose a good training school. I would recommend masters with experience to learn unceasingly, and always strive for new knowledge. Approach this issue responsibly. By getting quality basic knowledge, you save several years on the road to perfection. Success is gained by those who are doing something every day to achieve it! If I could advise only one thing – it would be to never stop, to keep on setting challenging goals and keep on achieving them. It may not all come at once, sometimes you will have failures along the way, but you should not give up. Demonstrate your creative imagination, do not hesitate to show others what you can do. Be sure to take part in contests - this is the path to your vocation, a big step towards the development of your career. If you will need my help, I am always ready to suggest, help and advise. In my eyelash school I have trained many masters, and I say to each of them, that in order to achieve good results, you need to grow and develop (to attend advanced training courses, seminars, conferences). Without this, success will not be achieved. The well-known saying that "slow and steady wins the race" works, even in such a fine industry, as eyelash extensions.

I am inspired every day by the happy faces of my clients, the many words of gratitude I receive, the sparkling eyes of my students, and my prospects for the future. I also draw strength and inspiration by the wonder I see in the world, by having loved ones close to me, the ability to see, hear and explore our wonderful planet, and by my ability to see the extraordinary in the ordinary.

http://www.lash.lg.ua

Chapter 5

Stefani
ALTIERI

My name is Stefani Altieri, and I'm proud to be the owner of New Jersey's first continuing education program, Skyn Lash Academy in Howell, NJ. It has been a long road, full of ups and downs, successes and failures, and many mistakes along the way. I was able to learn from my mistakes and climb a ladder to success. I feel incredibly honoured to be able to write my life story to share with you all. I truly believe we can all learn from each other, and grow as a team.

I started my first job at 14 years old, working at McDonalds, and have been working hard ever since. I feel like I have had almost every job possible. From working as a shampoo girl, to corporate America project management, and many other jobs in between. I was always creative and good with my hands. I attended West Virginia University from 1990-1994, studying both nutrition and business management. I always had an artsy side, willing to try anything. I was often waxing or doing my friend's nails! I developed good business sense from working as a headhunter in a personnel agency, as well as working managing schedules and a trial prep in a large law firm in NJ.

It was my last job at a Wireless Communications Company as a Project Coordinator and Manager that convinced me that the corporate business world just wasn't for me. It was my dream at the time to one day have my own business, I just wasn't exactly sure what I wanted to do. I got married in 1996 and had a beautiful son, Jake, in 2003.

In 1999, I left the corporate world and worked temporarily at a friend's hair salon at the front desk. I decided to purchase a busy tanning salon named Sunquest. Sunquest had been in business for 8 years before I decided to buy it. When I first purchased Sunquest, the salon was very dated and as I like to call it a "hot mess". I opened a business line of credit and purchased all new updated equipment and poured my blood, sweat and tears into transforming Sunquest - giving it a much needed "makeover". Since I took over Sunquest, I was able to quadruple its earnings in a 4 year period.

In 2005, I purchased a tanning distribution company "Sunflow" in a 7000 square foot warehouse, with the hope that it would make enough money so that my husband could leave the construction business and help out with the distribution company. It was also at this time that the tanning industry took a huge financial hit. The negative media attention, and the new tan tax on top of the generalised economic state of the country at this time made business extremely difficult. Long story short, the people who sold me "Sunflow" sold me essentially a non-existent business. It was here that I learned the most valuable business lesson and ended up in the middle of a large lawsuit - with my lawyer who did not do his due diligence in representing me. Tanning is a very seasonal business. It was always the top priority for me to carry and utilize the best of the best in the industry (This still remains a priority of mine). I decided to begin spray tanning and began attending the tanning trade shows. I met someone at a Tanning Trade Show in Nashville, who recommended I attend ISPA (International Spa Conference). ISPA is where I fell in love with the spa industry - it was a trade show like no other - it's basically where I fell in love and found my calling. It was at this time, still 2005, that I became determined to turn Sunquest into one of the best combination Day Spa & Tanning Salons. In order for me to make this work, I had to turn Sunquest into a much more serious day spa. I felt it had to look like a day spa, not just a tanning salon, and carry serious skin products that yield results. I've seen almost every single beauty salon that added spa services fail in that department. I felt that the physical environment was one of the most important factors, especially in order to create the right atmosphere for people to want to get a facial or a massage in a tanning salon.

Eventually, I hired a massage therapist, an esthetician and acquired a reputable and serious skin care line and business was going well. This was when I was first introduced to Lash Extensions. In my quest to find a good esthetician, I had someone respond to my advertisement and asked if I would be interested in bringing lash extensions to Sunquest. She was a hairdresser that had just started doing lashes. This was also when I first started to have lash extensions on myself and I have had them ever since. It was at this time I was also going through a divorce, and instead of falling into a depression, I decided to take all my energy and started to build Sunquest Tanning and Day Spa. I was always a very hands on owner and passionate about everything I was doing. Eventually, I expanded the Day Spa business to another location.

Skyn the Day Spa was born and I took this opportunity to grow. In the long run, it brought me much success in the spa business, however the tanning industry was going downhill. After being fed up and frustrated relying on other estheticians and employees, I decided to attend school myself and get my skin care license. As a single mother, running 2 businesses and going to school was not easy. I attended school 5 days a week (9-5), and straight from school to do clients at the spa in the evenings. I still had a son to raise as well as 2 businesses to run. It was the longest, most gruelling 6 months of my life, but also the most rewarding. I acquired my license. I learned more than I could have imagined and this is where I actually developed tremendous respect for education in this industry. It was also around this time, that the esthetician who was working for me, trained me in lash extensions. I was unsure whether I would have the patience to sit there lashing very tediously. In just one day, she showed me the technique and I was thrown into lashing. I have to say, lashing came very naturally to me and I picked it up very quickly. My first time trying, I was actually very impressed with myself! I was also surprised by my skills and the fact that I actually enjoyed lashing. I also think my being a lash client every 2 weeks for 2 years made a huge difference on picking it up so quickly. Being a client was actually very beneficial to my learning lashing. I actually found lashing therapeutic. After a few years of lashing, I then decided to pursue my certification. It was at this time I realized that trainers in the lash industry left a lot to be desired. Education was always a priority for me. I loved attending various trade shows, and always enrolled for classes on the newest skin techniques, and this passion for education spilled over to lashes.

I always had the utmost respect and admiration for my father, Lawrence Liebowitz. He was loved and respected as a boss, a partner, a friend, and most of all as a dad. He was my mentor, and I always consulted him for support and guidance, and sometimes even financial support. In 2010, I suffered the greatest loss I can imagine. I lost my father. It changed my life in the blink of an eye, and ruined my family. It also taught me many life and business lessons. My father would always tell me, that I should stop killing myself working 24/7 and go work for someone else so that I could be a better parent, a better family member and enhance my personal life. After my father died, that is simply what I did. I locked the doors of all the businesses, and decided to take a step back and go work for someone else. It was important to me that I work for an upscale successful salon & spa. So,……….

Once upon a time I went to work for a ruthless, evil cold-blooded Salon & Spa Owner. The owner of this salon I went to work for literally reminded me of an evil stepmother. For the purposes of this story we will use the fictitious name "Buddha". She treated her employees (Cinderella's) like garbage, yelling, screaming and being very cruel. She only cared about the money coming in, and was not concerned with the best interest of her employees or the clients. For example….I could not comprehend if the client came in for a "Skinceutical Facial" —we were not given all the Skinceutical products to perform the facial. We had to use low quality generic products for most of the facial, and only a few of the promised Skinceutical products. I found it both fraudulent and unethical. The day to day operations of that salon and spa were so unethical and inhumane, I was actually shocked at the employee retention. Truth be told I actually made a lot of positive changes for "Buddha", especially when it came to lashing. They were actually using lashes and tools from a very well-known company, however they were somewhat behind the times and not up to date with the industry. I was able to bring the best high quality products and tools with me to use on my clients at the salon. I never got recognition for anything positive I did there, in fact a certain co-worker would usually take credit for my ideas. She would then throw me under the bus at any given opportunity in order to make herself look better. I slaved for 2 years too long at "Buddha"... we fought constantly because I had a difficult time being forced into dishonesty.....it simply is not in me. I pride myself on being honest and straight forward, something I felt I was not able to do working for "Buddha". It was during this time I learned that there are both dishonest and unethical business owners and employees. It was quite an eye- opening experience. Once I left "Buddha" I felt that the suffocating bag over my head was released --and I was able to breathe again and get back to my creative, motivated self. The possibilities were endless. It was time to follow my dreams. I tried on a new pair of shoes, and the glass slipper fit.....I was off to start my own business....again.

I took courses offered by the BAALA (Be an Amazing Lash Artist) and the Lash Mastery Group in December 2012. These courses gave me the tools and education to help become a certified Master Lash Educator and Trainer. During the time that I participated in many classes and seminars on both skin and lashes, I realised that there was something missing. I felt that there was a tremendous lack of continuing education services being offered to professionals in the business. I then made it my personal mission to develop a Training Academy in an effort to help others further their education and training. This Academy would also house an actual studio where the students can always return -- for either support, guidance or more continuing education.

In an effort to continue my education at the highest of levels, I also attended the Lashboom Conference in Chicago in June 2013. I wanted to learn the newest technique in the lash industry which was then Volume Lashing. It was at this conference that I met Adele Sutton, and fell in love with Adele's products. During her training, Adele asked me to be the Master Trainer and Distributor for Lashcoat in the United States. I was so honored by this gesture that I decided it was time to expand my business to a larger training studio, in order to ensure success in these new and exciting ventures.

I was also trained and certified (Hands On) in the latest trend of Volume Lashing by Olga Volkova, the original creator of the "Hollywood Technique", Head of Lash Art University and LashMaker Magazine from Russia, Kiev, & Ukraine; Nadia Afanaseva from X VIP Lashes in Russia, and Teresa Smith, Master Lash Artist in London and the author of The Lash Bible from the United Kingdom.

I participated and have also been certified in the Advanced Technique of Volume Lash Extensions as well as Brow

Architecture Design from the Lash & Brow Design Academy (Moscow, Russia), from Irina Levchuk, President. I also hosted Irina's courses at my Studio in Howell, NJ and was able to spend 5 full days with Irina which was an invaluable experience. I was able to develop great insight into this challenging technique and it helped me to really grasp the concept and skills needed to achieve the perfect volume.

Every time I completed a class or training, I would come back to the studio and begin to implement the new techniques I had learned. I would always wish however, that there would have been a way that I could go back to my trainer to ensure I was utilising the techniques that were taught to me effectively and correctly. Most classes that I attended required me to travel outside of New Jersey. Often, it was the trainer that traveled from city to city in order to educate the students in that area. As a matter of fact, there was no real advanced schooling in and around my home state of New Jersey.

There is a big difference between properly and improperly applied eyelash extensions. In order to increase consumer confidence and to help other Lash Artists in the industry, I became certified with ADFEE (Association for Damage-Free Eyelash Extensions) as an Exam Proctor & Master Lash Artist. I am honoured to be the first Master Esthetician/Master Lash Artist in the State of New Jersey to hold this respected certification. ADFEE is "an independent association of advanced lash technicians who are passionate about proper application and delivering the highest ethical standards in the industry of Eyelash Extensions". ADFEE Exam Proctors personally evaluate each lash extension is applied to a single, natural lash and that applicants are delivering the highest quality and safety standards in eyelash extension application.

Skin and Lash Studio & SkynLash Academy were born in late 2013. My vision had come true. The continuing education classes that were lacking in this industry could now be right around the corner. We offer training courses in Lash Extensions from the Basic to Advanced/Design to Volume, Lashcoat and Spray Tanning. My goal for the future is to incorporate advanced skincare and Laser/IPL classes at my facility as well. It's been a very rocky road with many speed bumps...but I just keep moving full speed ahead. In November 2013, I flew to Hong Kong and attended Cosmoprof, the Biggest Beauty Trade Show in the world, with a goal of seeking the best lash supplies. I asked myself: where else am I going to get an opportunity to physically touch, feel, and see so many lash suppliers at one time in order to find the quality products in person? It was also important for me to be able to meet the suppliers of these products and begin developing a positive relationship with them.

I also have become a wholesale distributor to licensed beauty professionals, offering a wide variety of all high quality lashes and eye enhancement supplies. In all my years of lashing, I felt there were several really important features missing in the lash products. This process is taking a lot longer than I had originally anticipated because I won't just settle on anything that has my name on it. I have to only use the best of the best. It's extremely time consuming to do this the correct way. It's back and forth experimenting, researching and physically trying and using almost every brand of lashes, adhesives, eye pads, and tweezers. I am very detailed and OCD-like with things that I am very passionate about.

I am proud to announce my newest baby Stella Lashes. I am so excited and cannot wait to launch my new brand lash line around the world. I should also mention that I offer medical esthetic services for clinical corrective skincare for visible results. Skin care is another passion of mine and I find great enjoyment in correcting and transforming my client's skin and making women feel beautiful. I offer dermaplaning, microderm, chemical exfoliation, IPL Laser treatments for corrective skin treatments and hair removal as well as spray tanning in addition to the lash and brow services. Brow courses are next on my agenda to offer as I have recently completed an online intensive Brow Course by Brow Artists International. This has made me look at brows in a whole new light and it has become my new passion! (brows really used to scare me!)

The last thing I would like to discuss are my inspirations and my greatest motivations in this business. Inspirations include but are not limited to Olga Volkova, creator of Vivienne Premium Eyelash Extensions, head of Lash Art University & LashMaker Magazine and creator and owner of Lashboom World Lash Education Conferences. Olga runs a salon, trains, and distributes the first ever Lash magazine. She also has her own lash line that I seek to emulate. Olga has also sponsored, judged and facilitated many Lash Competitions. I believe Olga is very well respected in this industry, and she is both sweet and kind. She doesn't have a mean bone in her body. Olga is very intelligent and has the same passion and work ethic that I have. I have tremendous admiration and respect for Olga, and hold her in the highest regard. My main goal for the future is to help build a better lash industry and help the industry get a more positive reputation by raising the quality of the industry standards.

I also would like to give some advice to new lash artists just starting out in the business. My greatest wish is that new lash artists would learn that slow and easy wins the race. In my opinion, the biggest mistake made in this industry is that new lash artists want to be trained so quickly. Everyone is looking for a one day, short, inexpensive trainings. Honestly, lashing is an art and a highly detailed technique that requires much skill, and takes serious time and a lot of work - training should be spread out over a period of 3 to 5 days for basic techniques. Some advanced artistry can be learned in 1 day for seasoned Lash Artists. However, Volume lashing is definitely not an easy technique to grasp and perfect and I do believe at least 2

- 3 days of training are necessary in most circumstances. The biggest complaint I hear from lash artists are that they felt they did not get enough training or information at their first one day lash training class. There is far too much information, in addition to learning a very difficult technique to absorb in one day. It takes a tremendous amount of practice to perfect this technique.

One last major tip I would like to mention is something not everyone may believe. I strongly feel that if you are offering and providing a service for a client (no matter what it may be), it is extremely beneficial that you have received this service yourself. There is no better way of learning about being a service provider than being an actual client yourself. This certainly assists you in understanding your clients' needs more effectively. In turn, making you a better service provider or technician. I can't stress this enough. It often bothers me when I see lash artists who have said they have never had lashes before. There are many ways to become a client in your own industry, you can either pay for the service directly from another technician, or you can even seek out another professional in your area to possibly barter services with. I also recommend going to other salon's and spas and get facials, spray tans, lashes, or whatever services you provide. Be aware of other salons and spas around you, the services they offer, and techniques they use. You can learn a lot from visiting other salons. It can often be eye-opening and motivating at the same time.

In almost every one of my courses offered, whether they are 2 or 3 days in a row of training, there is an additional day built into the course to allow students the opportunity to return to the studio for the last day of training. This last day of training occurs a month or two after they have been out on their own, practicing their new skills and techniques. This gives me a chance to now see what they have been doing, measure their progress and help critique and correct any issues that come up. This also gives my students another hands on day with me to go over any questions and concerns that they are having. One thing I am most passionate about is that I wish I had been offered this opportunity to have my trainer correct and help me to perfect my technique and make sure I am doing everything the proper way. The best lash artists are those that have taken their time to learn correctly. You simply cannot be prepared to lash clients after receiving a couple hours of training in one day. I also believe it is important to revisit techniques and trainings to refresh or perfect skills necessary in this industry. I strive to make that a benefit of the Skin & Lash Academy. Students are always welcome to come back to the studio to practice, correct, or refresh their techniques and have questions answered. I am now so excited that **NEESA**, National Eyelash Education & Safety Association has been born. It is much needed for this Industry. I am proud to be nominated as a Board Member and hope that I will be selected to assist the Board in making the necessary positive changes in our industry. I feel strongly about continuing education and know the need to have a higher quality of training is desperately needed in the lash industry. This year North America is having its first ever Lash Competition, one of which I have been given the honour of being a First Time Judge at: Lash Wars in Vegas in June 2014. This competition is created and hosted by NEESA.

I am also beginning to develop a business aspect to all of my trainings. Each training will have time set aside to discuss business do's and don'ts, and I will be there to support those students looking to launch their own business. My success is their success. I highly recommend that all lash artists, technicians and anyone in this industry get as much continuing education and training as possible from many different educators and trainers in order to become a well-rounded professional lash artist. I want to help my students be the best that they can be. If you say you can't afford continuing education, the truth is - YOU CAN'T AFFORD NOT TO!!!

I would not have been able to develop my successful business without the help of some of my family members. I already mentioned my father, without his support and guidance I am not sure if I would have gone down this path of practicing what I love. My mother also continues to support me in so many ways, and I can't thank her enough for supporting me in achieving my dreams. I thank God for my mother in law who is always there for me to help me with my son in order for me to make my business a success.

LASH MASTERS

I believe education and knowledge are the keys to a successful business in any industry. I am passionate about teaching, strive for excellence and I am determined to keep up with the latest and greatest trends in this industry without compromising quality. I hope to keep all of my students one step ahead, while providing them a platform to return to a professional environment of education and practice, whenever they may need it.

> "Being able to help other people & to help achieve their personal goals gives me great pleasure!"

Stefani Altieri

SkynLash Academy
2224 US Highway 9
Howell, NJ 07731
731-618-2096
www.skynlashacademy.com
www.the-lash-shop.com
www.skinlashstudio.com

Chapter 6

Britta **KRUEGER**

Britta Krueger, Founder and Owner of Flirties Products and training ltd.

After being involved in the beauty industry for almost twenty years, (through working with various brands within WOW FACTOR and Beautytrix) we have seen many product and treatment ideas come and go. None however, have been so exciting as Lash Extensions, nor offered such a wide range of enhancements to show off the skills and creativity of a true professional.

As this Lash Masters book already contains a range of chapters from lash technicians and artists, I thought it might be interesting to write about the other side......How products evolve, are manufactured, launched and used for training professionals.

When we first started playing with the idea of eye enhancements, and lash extensions in particular, it was a brand new thought which seemed a bit bizarre at first, and

I do admit that, whilst I thought it was an exciting new treatment to create a fabulous look; I also guessed it would be more of a specialist clientele who would benefit: i.e. brides, prom nights, special occasions and holidays for anyone who wanted to have a stunning set of lashes, without the trouble of having to apply mascara or other products on a daily basis.

It is hard to believe that there is now a whole new market relating to just these enhancements which include

- Lash and brow tinting and shaping
- Brow design
- Brow extensions
- Semi-permanent mascara
- Lash Lifting
- Quick Fix Lash Trix
- Express lash application
- Semi-permanent lash extensions
- Advanced lash techniques including speed lashing and glamourizing
- Advanced volume technique with 2D – 6D sets

and the list keeps growing, as creativity of lash artists and manufacturers continue to strive for better application methods, advanced techniques and more efficient products and tools.

Since we first launched Flirties we have taken great care to develop products which are specifically designed for this application, and we only use medically approved adhesives to ensure the safety of client and therapist as well as efficiency and reliability.

We firmly believe in offering our customers the best quality products at affordable prices and combined with our fully accredited training throughout the UK and Ireland, this provides the key for therapists being able to offer a superior treatment.

Over the years Flirties has made a name for itself and been voted "best product" through various media for many years in a row.

All our educators are therapists which enables us to continuously look out for possible improvements, new product ideas and also to take in feedback from other therapists. This also allows us to watch over the quality through our own experience in addition to the quality checks of the strict ISO guidelines which the specialist testing laboratories demand.

It is challenging to find new and improved ways forward in order to support our customers, and it takes a lot of dedication and passion in order to work with great enthusiasm on a daily basis but the whole Beautytrix team has grown together so strong that it is more fun than work – not many people are able to say that about their job!

We all need each other and Flirties is what it is due to the hard work everyone involved has put into this. I am enormously grateful to be working with such a skilled, creative and loyal team and over the years we have all become friends as well as respecting each other as colleagues, educators and therapists. The strength of a team has to be "one for all and all for one".

We see many students pass through our doors, from those who come for basic training from scratch with no prior knowledge or qualifications, to those who come for advanced training or tutoring to improve their skills and offer clients different treatments and techniques. It is very rewarding when we can teach someone the necessary skills, and then see that therapist set up in business and make it a success. We love helping and getting involved not only in the actual treatment procedures but also with background knowledge regarding customer care, marketing and how to increase client base or improve profit margins. It is such a great feeling to know that you have been able to support someone in creating a successful business.

Lash applications can be quite tricky to learn but it is amazing to see someone evolve from the first time they pick up the tweezers (and are ready to throw them in a corner out of frustration!) to then becoming a very skilled therapist and lash artist who thinks about lashes day and night. Many of our students become addicted to transforming client's lashes and become highly skilled and knowledgeable, developing a finely trained eye for determining which technique and products to use for the best look. The range of available options is so vast that it takes a good therapist to suggest and perform the treatment; whether it will be a natural set of beautiful lashes or an exaggerated glam set which will enhance client's features or eyes and make them stand out and sparkle. If done correctly those treatments can work miracles in enhancing your client's positive features.

The Beauty Industry now offers endless opportunities to set up in business and you can be your own boss or work in a salon with hours to suit your lifestyle and family commitments. From our own experience and those of our customers and students over the years, we would like to give a word of advice to anyone taking this step and starting a new venture, whether it will be starting your own business or adding a new treatment to your portfolio: Training and products are the key to success! Without the fundamental knowledge and skills you can't succeed and your treatments will never be earning you praise or be outstanding. With this in mind, make sure you look for thorough training from a renowned and fully accredited provider, to ensure you learn things from scratch. Unfortunately many students think they can cut corners and either attempt to learn by video or youtube or they try and save money by booking an overcrowded course – in both cases you might find that you have to invest more time and money this way than booking the right course from the beginning. The same advice can also be said for products, as a perfect technique won't achieve outstanding results without high quality products! Don't try and save a few pennies on one of your essential products. Shop wisely and calculate what a pound or two difference actually means per treatment - you will be surprised that it will only mean a few pence difference. Do you really want to risk your reputation, your business, and potentially yours and your client's health for a few pence by cutting corners and buying products that might not be suitable for the treatment or may not be approved for use in your country? Your work and your clients health and safety should mean more to you so don't risk it! Try and make your life easier by using quality tools. Have you ever tried to pick up lashes with bent tweezers? You will be trying that for a long time so don't waste your time with inefficient tools – money wisely spent means commercial gain!

Take pride in your work and give 100% at all times. Be passionate about the treatments you offer – only this way will you be able to stand out from your competition. Don't enter into a price war and undersell yourself or your treatments – it's a downward spiral and no one wins as you are competing for pennies and eventually you will work for nothing, and be forced to cut corners with inferior products which results in a vicious circle and will not win you clients. Know your worth and charge it! Stand out from the competition through the use of quality treatments and products and offer your clients a service they are happy to pay for!

LASH MASTERS

Don't be disheartened if it seems difficult or even impossible at the beginning! Everyone has started at some point and even the most advanced lash artists will be able to tell you how they were ready to throw in the towel (or tweezers) at the beginning. Practice, practice, practice, and if you are unsure ask your trainer for some more time or tutoring to go through the areas you are unsure about or those you want to improve, and you will see that it will all fall into place.

If you are setting up your new business don't give up if clients aren't queuing at your door straight away! Every business takes time to grow, but if you persevere and use the marketing tools that are known to work then it will all happen! (It just takes a bit of time and patience).

For more help and advice on all lash related matters you can also have a look at our Flirties Guide To Lash enhancements A-Z which will be released shortly.

And now it's time to have some fun so pick up your tweezers and lashes and see where creativity can get you!

Flirties Products and Training ltd.
Unit 2/3 Tarlair Business Park
Tarlair Way, Macduff, AB44 1RU
Tel. 0845 022 2233
www.flirties.co.uk

Chapter 7

Kathryn **POPPLESTONE**

Hi lash lovers, I'm Kathryn Popplestone, the founder and co-owner of the Flutter Franchise. We are a team of highly skilled mobile eyelash extension specialists. I'm passionate about lashes and absolutely love what I do. Hopefully you will find the following chapter useful to you if you are looking to start your own business, move into the industry or simply improve your skills.

I started my Flutter business on August 8th 2008 because I saw 2 niches in the market:
1. Salon quality mobile service.
2. Team of consistent high-quality artists who specialise solely in lashes.

I decided to Franchise as it is the best way to maintain quality and give individuals the opportunity to work for themselves with both extensive lash training and business support.

Our 1st Franchisee started in 2011 and 3 years later we now have a highly performing team of 20 'Flutterettes' including

14 Franchisees. We are really proud of our amazing team who all work exceptionally hard to support each other. They have their own territory areas, so are not in competition with each other. We are the exclusive brand at the Urban Retreat mega salon in Harrods and have been for over four years. The flutter service is also available at the Dorchester Spa and we have recently launched at the Josh Wood, Atelier Beaute.

A Little Background on Me

I studied both biochemistry and nutrition before starting Flutter. I also worked as a nail technician alongside my studies from 14 years of age. I had always had a keen interest in art and I loved the transformation you could create with nail treatments, especially the sculpted French acrylic nails which were so popular back then. I also loved experimenting with nail art and have always enjoyed fine detailed work.

I first trained in lash extensions in August 2005, when lashes first became available in the UK. I was intrigued with eyelash extensions as soon as I heard about the treatment. I wasn't blessed with great natural lashes. They are fine and very straight so I was constantly curling them and applying layer after layer of mascara trying to create more length and volume. When I saw a lash training course advertised I thought 'All women want longer, thicker, fuller lashes, I have to do this training!' I have been wearing lash extensions myself ever since and couldn't be without them for even a week! I loved the service from that first day, but the products and technique were very basic. The adhesive was painfully slow to dry and only 1 type of curl (J curl) and thickness (0.10mm) were available, making the choice of looks very limited as well as the treatment time extremely long. After spending two and a half hours applying lashes nearly all would fall within two weeks!

In a quest to be able to offer a treatment that created a mascara effect that could be worn on a continuous basis, I did trials with hundreds of different products while perfecting my application technique. At this point very few people offered a lash service, so there were few resources to find information and advice like there is today. It took a lot of self-teaching through trial and error, mostly on my poor, long suffering Mum! By the time I finished my Biochemistry degree and moved back to Surrey I had found products and a technique that created the look of mascara but better. Plus by this stage the adhesive choice had greatly improved, meaning the lashes lasted well so the client would have at least 60% retention after 3 weeks, making it viable to lie down for hour long infills, as well as giving a more consistent look between appointments.

At this point I started working in a prestigious hair & beauty salon in Mayfair, called Michael John, where I specialised solely in lash extensions. I have always believed that if you want to be the very best at what you do, you should specialise. Being an expert and choosing a niche means that clients will always be willing to pay a higher price for your service as the perceived value is greater. After only a few months I was fully booked and didn't even have time for lunch! A lot of people kept saying it was hard to find a consistent quality of service across one particular brand, making it hard to know who to trust that could perform a high quality service. A lot of people also expressed an interest in having an at home service offering more flexible times, especially as most salons at this point only opened Tuesday to Saturday 9am-6pm.

After doing some research I found a very lightweight but high quality mobile massage bed and portable light. This meant it was viable to be able to offer a salon quality lash service but in a client's own home and Flutter was born from this concept.

I started with just myself and one other Lash Artist, Zahara, covering the South West London and Surrey areas. We quickly built a strong loyal client base and took on 2 more Lash Artists. We also became the exclusive lash brand in the Urban Retreat Salon in Harrods and have now been there for four years. At this point we decided the best way to continue to expand the brand but maintain the highest and most consistent quality of service was to Franchise. This would give each of our lash artists the opportunity to own their own business under the Flutter name. They would have their own exclusive territory and the opportunity to earn a very good salary in the beauty industry.

LASH MASTERS

The Flutter Franchise

Our first franchise started in August 2011 and we now have a team of 20 Lash Artists covering a large part of the UK.

All of our franchisees go through very advanced training before they start their business so they are an expert in lashes before they even launch. Our training is the most comprehensive on the market with them completing 8 full days initial training spread over a 2 month period, completing 30 case studies, as well as a very difficult written and practical assessment before they are allowed to start trading. What also makes us unique is that we provide business training and support as well. It is all well and good being a great lash artist but if you don't know how to market yourself, and attract and retain customers then you won't have a successful business. After the initial training period we provide further advanced training, including techniques such as the new volume lashes as well as regular phone/face to face meetings and personal help at events to support their business growth.

All of the team have their own exclusive territories, so they are very happy to work together and support each other as there is no competition. They can be confident that any client that sees a Flutter Lash Artist anywhere in the country will receive the same high quality service as they provide themselves, further strengthening the brand. They can work together on promotions and can cover each other's clients for holiday or sickness. This gives them confidence to know their client won't need to see another lash artist, whose work may not be up to standard.

As a brand, we work hard to stay at the forefront of the industry. We always research new products as well as application techniques. I spend a lot of time personally testing every product and new technique that becomes available. If I think that it will help advance our business we will implement it across the whole team. In addition to developing our own products and technique of volume lashes - called Infinite Lashes - we have recently created an eye make-up range, KATE STONE COSMETICS, which has been specifically chosen for lash extension wearers. We felt there was a gap in the market for high quality cosmetics to complement and enhance client's lash extensions. This includes crème shadows, so the lashes don't look dusty from powder types, mascara, sealer, oil free make up remover, brushes and a growth serum.

My Top Business Tips
Anyone can start a business, but it requires a lot of personal strength to make it a success. Be patient and remember that you will make mistakes. As long as you learn from these and move forward it isn't a negative. Be patient, everything always takes longer than you think and it's the hardest and most painful just before you are going to succeed so keep pushing and don't give up!

You've got to be tough as leather sometimes. Business can

be very hard on you emotionally and physically. If you want to be successful be prepared to work long into the night, be willing to give up your weekends and invest everything you earn into the business you love.

Believe in yourself and don't listen to too many people's different opinions, but don't be afraid to ask for advice in areas that you have less knowledge. Always, always, trust your gut; it may not be scientific but mine has always been right and I have always regretted not listening to it. Finally, do something you are passionate about. It's always got to be about more than just money. If you love what you do, then that will show through in the business that you build. Money is only the means to an end not an end in itself.

What Inspired Me to Start My Business?

I am motivated by seeing other women achieve success, especially in female orientated industries. My grandmother, who I greatly admired, started and ran three businesses in a time when it was unusual for women to take on this type of role. She even played in the men's local cricket team! She opened my eyes to the fact that we are very lucky to have the opportunities we do, in this country, to build something meaningful.

Our goal at Flutter is to inspire our team to pursue their dreams of building a successful business for themselves. My hope is our business model will also encourage others to continue to improve the standard of the Lash Industry as a whole. We need to demonstrate to clients that eyelash extensions are a safe and effective treatment for eyelash enhancement, which can be worn on a continuous basis, without causing any harm to the natural lash.

The best of luck to every one of you in your journey, I hope you found something in this chapter useful or thought provoking.

By Kathryn Popplestone
Flutter Eyes Franchising Ltd.
http://www.fluttereyes.co.uk
http://fluttereyesfranchise.co.uk/01372386312

Chapter 8

Suzette ZUENA

Beauty is ubiquitous. We can see it in people, nature and creations around us every day. But to really appreciate this surrounding beauty, one must first feel the beauty from within. As a Master Lash Artist I am privileged to help women release their inner beauty day in and day out.

My name is Suzette Zuena and I am the founder of <u>Lash House Beauty Boutique</u> located in Livingston, New Jersey. I began my career as a part-time receptionist in a salon, while attending the Fashion Institute of Technology (FIT) in New York City. I remember the joy I felt from seeing clients glowing from having their hair done, or a facial, or even a fabulous manicure and pedicure. Sure they were more beautiful on the surface, but they were also more confident, had a twinkle in their eye, and a bounce in their step. This was when I learned that beauty treatments are not superficial; they are empowering. I immediately became passionate about pursuing a career in beauty that would enable me to provide clients with instant beauty, inside and out.

My foray into the field in 2002 was as a certified esthetician at the same salon where I discovered my passion. From the start I really cared about and treasured my clients and wanted to be the best I could be, so THEY could be the best THEY could be. I therefore felt it was my responsibility to stay on top of new trends that would enhance the beauty regimens of my clients, making me their go-to beauty expert.

In 2005 I learned about eyelash extensions; let's just say I have a guardian angel. My co-worker from years ago came to visit me and asked me about this new "fad" in the beauty industry "lash extensions". I had no idea that was even possible, so she wrote XTREME LASH on the back of her business card (which I still keep in a special place to this day) and we said our goodbyes. Nobody in my area was doing them, and clients certainly weren't yet asking for them, but my instinct told me extensions were going to be hot! That night I called and spoke to this very sweet woman and I was booked for the training certification. Who knew at that moment it was destiny?? My future was mapped; I was going to make a beautiful living doing something that I LOVED! I couldn't wait to show my ladies what long flirty eyelashes would do to improve their look, to make them feel sexy, and enhance their overall self-esteem. I knew that once I did, they'd come back for more, and their friends would see their lashes and they'd come in too. What I didn't know was just how much they'd catch on, ladies were coming from Connecticut, and Philadelphia, Maryland, and this allowed me to build towards a future in everything lashes!

Once I started doing extensions, I was amazed that my passion reached an entirely new level. The sheer joy on clients' faces after I do a full set of lashes is the most satisfying part of my career. I love seeing how happy I can make a client after spending two hours transforming the look of their eyes. Lashes are a labor of love. They are a very intricate process and seeing how much they benefit a client makes my hard work very worthwhile. For me its instant gratification! I was never one to work on a project for long hours just for a "job well done" or a pat on the back. I absolutely love the reaction of an ecstatic client, I truly feel like I make a difference every day.

Hard work is not enough though on its own. You also have to care about your clients as much, if not more, than you do about yourself! Seriously! You cannot be selfish in this business. I remember in the beginning of my lash days I had a client who had been with me since the very start. She had a friend's wedding in Santa Fe that was being filmed for a wedding reality show. She was in the bridal party and decided to have lash extensions and I was excited to be able to do them for her. She worked in Manhattan and was coming to me after work. She was flying out early the next morning. Unfortunately there was a severe rainstorm and the traffic was horrible. She was supposed to be in to see me at 5pm and didn't arrive until 8:30. I remember how amazed she was that

I had stayed after the salon closed to do her full set. In my mind there was no other option. This was where that passion and care for my clients become all consuming! When you work in the beauty industry more than likely you find yourself always needing waxing or a manicure yourself. You're so busy accommodating clients that you leave yourself until last. But at the end of the day, I want to do the best I can not only for me, but more so for my clients. They are why I do what I do and the foundation of everything.

Gradually over time there was so much demand for eyelash extensions, that I took to them full-time. I provided my services at a variety of salons and became known as the leading specialist in "New Jersey." At one point I even rented space in a carriage house. My clients proved to be very loyal, following me from location to location. To this day I'm not sure how in such a short time I was able to become a wife, a mother and a lash master. All I can say is that a lot has been sacrificed; family, friends and personal time.

As excited as I was to start my own spa, it was also very scary. I was a wife and mother to my sweet daughter Isabella and my baby boy Luca who was still in my belly. Being pregnant and having a one-year-old and a family dependent on me didn't feel like the most secure time to make the plunge. However I also knew that there was never going to be the perfect time, there would always be a reason to say not now and I had to go for it and reach for my dreams. That is yet another key factor to my success. Having a solid vision and seeing it through. This was the moment I became proactive, I absolutely had to stop saying "one day, I would love to have a beautiful lash boutique", I let go of all the "what if's "that were going through my head. Funny thing is I never thought of failure, I just didn't know if there were enough hours in the day to be a mom, wife and now boss? Well. Failure was and continues not be to an option. There is no room for fear in success.

You see, being a successful business owner is a formula and not everyone has the right equation, I am lucky enough to have an amazing partner in life and in love and I call him Danny and he is daddy to my children. Without his eternal support and encouragement I don't think I would have been able to take my career to where I have. I really see all that has been achieved and I am excited for where we will take this venture. He is a man strong enough to encourage my ambition and passion. He was never intimidated by it but rather he worked with me to find solutions to ensure that we could raise our family and achieve our dreams. I must also say a big support came from my amazing parents. When Danny and I would struggle with our schedules and I had a client who I had to make an emergency early morning or late evening appointment; with the help of my parents and Danny all was possible. Without the support of my family - my core team - none of what I have achieved would be possible.

My vision for Lash House was to create an intimate, very

up-scale, spa oasis; where women could check-in their daily stress at the door and leave feeling like a pampered princess - invigorated, renewed, and empowered. My attention to Lash House's detail was at a level on par with the detail I apply to every set of lash extensions. From the crystal chandeliers, to heated beds, to the mirrored wallpaper, Victorian receptionist desk, glistening Brazilian cherry black wood floors, Lampe Berger fragrance system, customized music and unique, specialized, hand-selected beauty products, Lash House is a textural and aromatic experience unto itself.

Just as important was my team of professionals. I scouted out the best waxers, lash artists and estheticians in the region, offering them attractive and unmatched compensation packages, knowing my clients would demand the 'best-in-breed'. They needed to care about their clients as much as I do about mine, since anything less would be unacceptable. With the right talent in hand, and my willingness to advise them and invest in their training, I now have a team of lash artists, in addition to the best facials and waxing services in town.

Here at Lash House we offer a variety of lash services from classic extensions to the new volume technique, using only the best lash materials and innovative adhesive. Beyond extensions, we offer Tint and Curl, which is perming the lashes then tinting them jet black. This treatment is best for women who already have beautiful lashes and just want them to curl and appear darker. We also offer a high-end strip application, which is perfect for the 'gal on the go' or can be used for an event (usually one evening use). We are proud to use Yonka Paris skincare as I deem there is no better skin care line. However, to truly be the Lash House for "everything lashes," I am always researching industry developments – new materials, techniques, approaches, and more.

That being said, advancing your knowledge is imperative, hence I am embarking on a journey to British Columbia, Canada to be the first person in the United States offering eyebrow extensions, a natural extension to my business but also a vital one. This new technique will open the door to a world of new and wonderful possibilities; giving strength back to men and women who are battling cancer being the most crucial one, while at the same time helping those suffering from alopecia. As part of this community, I feel a responsibility to bridge the gap and share my wealth of knowledge.

In addition to remaining committed to staying on top of new developments in the beauty field, especially pertaining to eyelashes; I am also committed to building strong relationships with my clients. In fact, some of my clients today have been with me throughout my entire journey. Many of my clients have become good friends because I really care for them. The relationship between a lash master and client is very personal. After all, we spend up to two hours locked in a room together.

I often play the role of confidant, therapist and overall advisor, as my clients do for me in return.

To be the best I can be at building and nurturing my client relationships is so important to me, that I take the time to stay on top of beauty and lifestyle trends well beyond my area of expertise – be it fashion, accessories, hair styles, exercise routines, diets, restaurants, cosmetic surgery, movies, music, and even politics. The more rounded I am, the more able I am to form real lasting connections with my ladies. I find myself advising my clients on where to purchase "that special dress," or where to get a cosmetic procedure done, and the best restaurant for that special occasion. Being in an up-scale beauty field gives me access to women who know the best of the best and between staying on top of the "news" and being a good listener, my clients trust I have valuable advice.

Building strong relationships, providing the highest-quality experience and services, and showing that we care at Lash House is the part that came naturally to me. After opening my spa, I also had to learn some business skills that didn't come as naturally – marketing, employee hiring and management, inventory management, financial projecting, and more. I definitely enjoy the creative side of what I do far more than running the business, but with Danny's help and the willingness from the start to invest in top-notch technology, we've more than figured it out!

My clients, as well as bloggers and media consistently comment on how special Lash House is. I'm therefore excited and confident about beginning the next chapter of my journey, to expand the Lash House concept to more locations.

www.lashbeautyboutique.com
Suzette.lashhouse@gmail.com
973-992-4300
Lash House Beauty Boutique
250 South Livingston Ave
Livingston, NJ 07039

Chapter 9

Leah
LYNCH

Born and raised in suburbia to two successful entrepreneurs, I learned at an early age that I would one day own my own business. Maybe it's the fact that I'm a Scorpio, or maybe it's my Sicilian background, but my fiery personality and my passion and drive have always been my strongest personality traits.

After graduating from college with a degree in liberal arts (also known as nothing specific) and entering the working world as a car saleswoman, I quickly found myself disillusioned with my career opportunities. I began wallowing in my own self-pity, unfocused, directionless, and unsure of where life would take me. I remember sitting down with my mother and taking a career aptitude test, weighing up my options. It was liberating to write down my dream job's pros and cons on paper so that it could begin to take shape. I want to feel good about the work that I do, I wrote. I want to make other people happy; be creative and inspired; have flexible hours; have access to unlimited pay increases; and be in an industry where I can constantly grow and learn new things.

I knew, definitively, that I could never work in an office, that I did not want anything stiff or boring and that I could not tolerate anything that lacked artistic flair or passion. It wasn't until a few months later that the pieces fell together when, serendipitously, I was presented with the opportunity to attend the Catherine Hinds Institute of Aesthetics in Woburn, Massachusetts.

Very quickly, I realized that aesthetics was my calling. Ironically, upon my graduation, the first position that was offered to me was a sales position with an Italian skin care line. I'm pretty sure it was the allure of being on a plane to Italy within a month of my hire date that had me signing on the dotted line. But a year and a half passed and I realized that I had come out of sales only to go back to school to change careers and go right back into the career I had hoped to avoid. I needed something more artistically fulfilling, and so, after deliberation, I made one of the best choices of my professional life: I took my first risk.

Good fortune, as it happened, was on my side. I landed a position at one of the top 200 salons in America, conveniently located in the historic downtown of my hometown, where I first was known for my skills in brow artistry. There, I was introduced to eyelash extensions. It was 2006, and the concept of eyelash extensions had been introduced to the United States only a few years prior. We were very much on the cutting edge, and no one else in the area was offering the service. In fact, there were no trainers in the area at all, and we had to have the head scientist from Novalash flown in from Los Angeles to host a private training for the seven girls at our salon. After returning from the training, we were required to put lashes on six models before taking our first client, and I was the only one who completed the models in a reasonable amount of time and, therefore, the first lash artist to hit the floor in our busy salon

Almost immediately, my schedule was full of lash extensions. I practiced for eight to 12 hours a day, taking up to 10 clients, back-to-back. They say a professional career is rooted in the repetition of a craft; by that logic, I certainly honed my skills at lash artistry. Lash extensions is a very difficult service, I realize, and, luckily, I was born with remarkable dexterity and perfect vision.

My skills had really begun to improve after receiving my second certification in advanced lash extension, and I was very excited to be invited to enter the Novalash "Lash Off" Competition in 2011 to find the best of the best in lash artists across the country. That year, I won the "Fan's Choice Award" for Best Lash Artist. I was also nominated by Novalash to appear in Modern Salon Magazine, alongside only a handful of other beauty professionals, as a "Successful Inspiring Woman in the Beauty Industry" for 2011. One of the prizes for winning the contest was a PR rep and, later that year, I appeared in several magazines and had banner ads on multiple web sites and beauty-related newsletters through two popular industry magazines, Beauty Lunch Pad and Salon Today Magazine. After winning the contest, it was clear that, after eight years, I had outgrown my position at my salon.

After realizing that I had the kind of reliable following that could support me going out on my own, the plan started to take shape for creating my own business! In 2013, I entered the Novalash national contest yet again, and this time won the National Award for the Most Natural Lash Artist of the Year. I received the PR rep yet again, going into the first year of my new business. Exactly one year after leaving my previous salon, I opened the doors of Beautique Salon & Day Spa in quaint, historic downtown Newburyport, Massachusetts. (beautiquenbpt.com) Beautique is a high-end beauty boutique, specializing in luxury niche services, including, of course, lash extensions. After thoroughly analyzing all of the numbers, I realized that the profitability and reliability of clientele within the eyelash extension world was astounding and the tremendous opportunity that lash artistry provides for a young entrepreneur like myself is incredibly empowering.

Then, in June 2013, the biggest breakthrough in the industry hit North America: Volume Lashes! I discovered volume lashes through some international blogs and immediately became obsessed with learning this new technique. I began networking with girls from all over the world, travelling to meet the top trainers and award winners like Courtney Buhler from Sugar Lash and even cross country to meet Irena Levchuk from Lash & Brow Design Academy in LA. I sought knowledge and supplies from any and every source imaginable and I began a quest to become amazing at this revolutionary new technique. Volume lashes is a game-changer, a dream-maker, and one of the most genius ideas to hit the industry in the past seven years that I had been doing lash artistry. I knew immediately that there was a tremendous opportunity in this new sector and began practicing my volume lash skills on my clients for an average of four hours a day, five days a week.

One of my biggest concerns for the industry is maintaining safety and healthful practice. With the introduction of volume lashes comes the possibility for this very difficult and advanced technique to be attempted by those without a firm foundation in classic lashing skills. I live in a heavily saturated lash area and there are nail salons and other local competitors producing unattractive and unhealthy sets that bring down the reputation of the service locally and inevitability as a whole. With the negative press that lash extensions have received in the past I began to see an opportunity in the market for not only top notch training but more strict safety regulations, measures of safety and measures of professionalism. Thus LAROW was born! … as if I didn't already have a full plate!

LASH MASTERS

LAROW Beauty Group (created by squishing LAsh and bROW together, clever huh?) brings together the most comprehensive and all inclusive manual, (encompassing ALL lash techniques, tips, tricks and secrets collected from all corners of the lash world), thorough and customized training sessions, quality lashes, custom adhesives, resources for all the best of the best products from all the most desired sources and, most importantly, continuing steady access to thorough and up-to-date technical information and knock-your-socks-off high-definition training and support videos. I wanted to support not only the working lash artist, but all the hard-working trainers and distributors and manufacturers out there making our success possible. With the purchase of live or video training students gain membership to the website and a host of customizable promotional videos and visual images for use on social media and thorough email, newsletters, advertising or for showing clients during consults. Also available through LAROW Beauty Group are training videos on lash tinting and perming, HDX brow shaping/threading/tinting/extension, lash health and safety, business mentoring and business secrets revealed, and aids such as marketing and promotional calendars, consent form examples, contract templates and links and reviews for every kind of lash supply, accessory or complimentary piece of equipment imaginable. Pretty much everything you could think of, and probably a few things you never even knew existed!

Needless to say, my life revolves around eyelashes. Everything eyelashes. I consider myself very lucky to have found my calling in life, and to have been able to pursue my dreams. Remember that list I wrote down with my mother? I hit every box on my checklist, and even boxes I didn't know I wanted in my dream job - or, as I can now call it - my dream career.

I can say that it's not easy, and that the road is long and bumpy. You can't expect to have someone to hold your hand, and even your close friends and family are not going to carry you through it; you have to want it for yourself, and you have to be willing to do the work and not give up and not give in. You are going to plan events, and maybe no one will show up. You are going to have people who will tell you they will be there for you and then not come through. You are going to invest all you have in people, and they won't see the value: they may not feel the passion and they may not see the dream. No matter. You just keep your head up and your eyes to the horizon, and fight. Keep moving forward. Keep on keeping on! The beauty industry is an amazing industry that has grown through even the greatest of depressed financial times. Even now, in a bad economy, I can charge more for my time than most high-priced lawyers! There is always something new to learn, some new service or product to explore, and I find a genuine sense of accomplishment in making people beautiful. That is my career: changing the way people feel about themselves. We are lucky ladies, and we should embrace the opportunities before us, which allow us to be the powerful and successful women we are all destined to be. Whether you were inspired to read this book to further your successes within your career, to one day own a business of your own, or to improve your existing business, take a risk, think big and I can only hope that my story of success will serve as an inspiration that you can have what you dream!

www.larowbeautygroup.com

Beautiquenbpt@gmail.com

978-255-2774

Chapter 10

Francesca
MIDDLETON

Hi, my name is Francesca Middleton, and I run a lash business in the UK called LASH by Francesca, which incorporates a lash training school called the LASHacademy (LA), a private professional salon and a professional product range for lash technicians.

Before entering the lash industry I owned a consultancy business and had a business in fashion accessories and jewellery. Prior to that I worked in the corporate environment, specifically within the IT industry. You could say I was a bit of a geek, as I was responsible for software development and training of the IT consultants with the latest software technologies.

I have always loved my work, and although I have always worked long hours, I have had opportunities to travel internationally (which isn't as glamorous as it sounds!) and have won awards for my work contributions; I firmly believe these attributes were primal to setting up a successful lash business.

LASH MASTERS

I received my first lash training in 2006 and undertake to receive further lash training every year. I believe that we never stop learning and as trends come and go it's important to keep up to date with what's new.

I don't like to promote who I trained with first because the skills I have today are not a testament to one training company, but to all of them as well as a determination and desire to self learn. My self learning has been the biggest contribution to the quality of my lashwork and in engineering different but effective applications in creating artistic lashwork.

My fascination with lashes comes from not being graced with a natural long and full set of my own. When you have short, straight lashes, you don't face the world without first curling your straight lashes and then applying several coats of mascara to make you feel human!

So when I found an ad promoting eyelash extensions, I was instantly interested if not a little puzzled on how this could be achieved. All my hesitations instantly evaporated when after my first treatment, I blinked into a mirror with the most amazing set of lashes. I felt feminine, confident and very happy. It was love at first sight!

There was only one problem - The cost. I paid over £300 for them and like an addict looking for the next fix I wondered how I was going to be able to afford such an extravagant beauty treatment. My answer was simple, I would learn how to do them myself.

After booking myself onto a training course I discovered that [at that time] there were no case study requirements or assessments - you were instantly qualified. It seemed a little strange to me because half of the girls in my class couldn't grasp the application technique, and although I found it initially frustrating and awkward, I was lucky that my first set was considered good enough for a professional set.

It seemed like fate had held a hand because soon after I met a business angel and premises for my first salon. It was a very exciting time.

My business started in Chelsea, central London, and I had a fabulous launch party to celebrate, because at the time it was the only lash salon in the neighbourhood.

The salon was an instant success and I quickly became 'The Lash Lady' – the go-to girl from an exclusive clientele of society women, film and model celebs, and high profile professionals. I was soon travelling regularly to St Tropez and other amazing destinations, all in the name of lashes! From Chelsea, I also had a presence in Knightsbridge and Mayfair and was invited to work at Harrods, which I turned down because my vision was more than being a super successful lash artist.

In 2009, I launched the LASH professional product label and the LASHacademy (LA) to cater for students who wanted a personal and intensive training experience that would teach not only the basic application methods but also the elements on how to master lash artistry. We included mentoring through the student's skill journey as an important element to their training experience.

I'm very proud to say that the students who have completed the LA courses are all extremely talented and successful lashers. You'll be surprised at who has been through the LA. Many of the names and companies who inspire new lashers today came to the academy to fine tune their skills and pick my brains for business and lash advice!

In 2012 the LASHacademy (LA) was franchised out to lash trainers who wanted to learn the blueprint of firstly how to be a master lash technician, and then how to be an effective trainer and create a successful business for themselves.

Finally after many international lash professionals travelled to London to the LA this year, the LASHacademy went international, delivering training in South Africa with further training to Canada, United States, Australia and New Zealand all in the pipeline.

The business now is really more about how to help lash technicians build and enjoy the success of having a profitable lash business. I believe there is enough business for everyone and I am not worried about creating competition. It keeps me on my toes and ensures that my learning always strives to be at the next level.

I think in many ways I'm just like other lash professionals. I'm passionate about delivering an excellent set of lashes. I love when my clients open their eyes and they have huge smiles and gasps of 'thank you' for making them look gorgeous and feel confident.

I'm passionate about delivering training to allow the students to flourish with their newly acquired lash skills. I love it when my students 'click' with the new techniques and applications which will help improve their lashwork to their clients.

I'm passionate about providing the best products lash technicians can use in their treatments. It's important to keep the reputation of the treatment of lash extensions as high as possible because when it's done right it's the best treatment ever but when it's done badly it becomes the worst experience of your life!

However, what makes me different from other lashers is that I am very direct and blunt. To everyone. I'm told I'm not like other beauty professionals by my clients and students. To some sensitive souls, it's too much, but I am who I am and the people who know me, know that I always have the best of intentions and am always willing to help, almost like a tough love to make them the best they can be.

Setting up in business is very exciting and challenging and it goes without saying that it's an awful lot of hard work. Don't be fooled it's going to be easy. Be prepared to go that extra mile, give more of yourself and create customer loyalty. This will pay you dividends in the future.

Build yourself a great team and set of processes behind you. It doesn't matter if you're an independent lasher with no 'professional' team. It's about having the right people around you and the right processes in place to keep your customers happy.

For example, a great babysitter/mum if you need childcare. A reliable car if you provide on-location services. Whoever answers the phone – make sure they answer it in a happy professional manner. Don't be late and on the flip side have a late/cancellation policy and enforce it!

My last bit of advice is to respect your lash colleagues copyright in pictures and in text. With social media the world has become very small and any indiscretions will quickly get picked up. They say imitation is the greatest form of flattery but using other peoples work is quite frankly stealing and most professionals take a dim view of this. Look after your reputation.

As I've said previously, it's a small world, so conduct yourself with honesty and integrity because business is like karma, what goes around comes around. What you reap you sow. And whilst it's important to do this, don't expect everyone you come into contact to do the same or to have the same ethics and morals.

Listen to your gut, trust it and learn to act on it. Don't gossip! It's a small world and you'll be surprised who knows who. The last thing you want to be dealing with is petty gossip about 'he said, she said' scenarios. Concentrate your energy on building your business and creating positive success.

Your passion will show you the right way. I believe that the more passion you have, the more opportunities will become available to you.

I am inspired all the time by people in business, because it's people that make business.

I am inspired with amazing lashwork from fellow lashers. Lash work is really an art form and just like a painting I can find depth and mastery in outstanding lashwork.

I'm inspired by my students, who take on board my trainings and bounce off to create their own signature skill-sets.

And finally, I am inspired by my clients, each of them who

wear my art on their lashes, look after them and respect the skills needed to keep their lashes looking just fabulous all the time.

02033713513
francesca@lashbyfrancesca.co.uk
http://www.lashbyfrancesca.co.uk

Chapter 11

Zola
NEMORIN

With a long and impressive list of accomplishments in the professional beauty industry, as well as experiences in sales, finance, management, distributing, entrepreneurship, cosmetic formulating, database management, technical writing, graphic design, and training – you would never know that Zola wasn't always this successful. "We never know what God has in store for us," Zola says, "We learn from our life experiences, from difficult times. I didn't start my company, SKYN Clinic & Apothecary, when I was at the top of my game. I literally was emotionally and financially strained. I was looking for home remedies to fix my skin, and just trying to find myself, and what would make me happy." Her life experiences has served as an inspiration to thousands of beauty professionals as they strive to succeed in their own businesses and lives. Changing people's lives and helping them re-gain their confidence has become a personal mission for Zola, who strives to globally transform the spa industry. With Zola's leadership, SKYN Clinic & Apothecary has become one of the leading Non-surgical and Corrective centres in her country.

Born in Kingston, Jamaica, Zola comes from a large family

with many relatives; some as old as 90 years. Although she was not raised on the island, a lot of the Jamaican culture and traditions were passed down to her from her family members. "I remember my Dad making us drink blended lettuce, carrots, and parsley. We would always run away and think the drink was nasty." "My mom would force us to take cod liver oil pills, she said it would make our immune system strong." As an adult, Zola would later see her father's drink in a magazine, titled "Ways to clean your body out and lose weight". So, it is no surprise that she is so skilled at creating natural product formulations. Zola is a learner, it is actually more of a gift. "Learning has become a hobby for me, if I am not learning something new, or seeking new information, I feel useless to myself and the people around me." Zola comments, when asked why she has so many degrees. What Zola did not know about a subject, she made up for by becoming an ongoing learner throughout her life. She has attended over 500 hours in seminars, conferences, and classes with some of the world's most well-known and respected beauty and business professionals. Zola also holds an MBA with a concentration in Finance, a Bachelor Degree in Fine Arts, and an Associate Degree in Computer Science, as well as numerous certificates in Business Development and Planning, Medical Esthetics, Nail Technology, Semi-permanent Eyelash Extensions, Cosmetic and Natural Cosmetic Formulating, and Permanent Make-up. To top it all off she is currently a candidate for the Naturopathic Doctoral Program. Zola states, "I am only as good as what I know. I always tried to surround myself with people who knew more than I did, people that I could learn from."

While Zola undoubtedly excels in her knowledge, she attributes something else as the greatest motivation for her success – working with her hands. "I think of myself as having gifted hands," she states. She loved to create and fix things with her hands. As a child Zola would often 'fix' electronic equipment around the house, taking apart VCR's and putting them back together - always making sure she fixed them correctly before her parents realized what she had done. All of these intricate processes taught her how to pay attention to detail, how to do things with finesse and ease, how to correct and fix things, and most of all how to have patience. These are skills that she still practices today in her company, and while working on clients. Zola says, "applying eyelash extensions is not an easy task, and is not for everyone. You have to learn to work diligently, but carefully, and it is a must that you have patience". Zola has always had a knack for fixing things and helping others. At the age of 10, she started her first company, selling candy to the kids in her neighborhood. In a short period of time Zola's little candy stand grew into a large operation. "Every two weeks, I would have to take her to Sam's to re-stock on candy. My doorbell rang every second, with children coming from other subdivisions coming to buy Zola's candy" her mom says. Zola saw the need in her small town of Union City, GA and she filled the demand, at such a young age. This is where her entrepreneurship skills began. Zola's first regular paying job was at Burger King. She quickly became one of the best employees, learning how to make the food and work the cash register. "I learned how to run the whole restaurant, and could single handedly run the meat grill and take orders. People thought we had a whole staff in the building, sometimes, it was just the manager and I," Zola laughs. This is where she received a crash course in customer service and the assembly line, which is what she refers to as her 'Six Sigma' training. With her Burger King job, Zola was able to buy her first car at the age of 15, with all her own money. "I saved all the money that I made from Burger King that summer, and on my birthday, my mom took me to buy a car. That was a big deal for me. For the first time I could physically see what happens when you work hard."

While away at college, having a lack of funds began to take a toll on Zola, as it would any college student. "At that time I was addicted to getting my nails done, as most of the young ladies were at my age." "When you're a starving college kid, you can't waste your money on manicures, you have to eat, so I started doing my own nails." "I realized that the other girls in my dorm had the same issue as I had, hence the idea of dropping out for a semester to get my nail license was born", noted Zola. She didn't inform her parents of her semester long vacation, which upset her parents when they found out, and it also delayed her esthetics course work. "Of course my parents were livid when they received the bill from the International School of Skin and Nail Care, so after completing the nail program, I decided to hold off on my esthetics license," Zola said with a grin. Obtaining her nail license was just the beginning of her adventure in to the beauty industry. Zola realized that she could use her hands again, creating and fixing things, while making a profit at the same time. She has worked in every facet of the nail industry from working on celebrities, to working in the corner nail shops, to five diamond spa resorts; picking up knowledge and skills wherever she went.

Zola excelled at her first career job, as a receptionist for a Non-profit organization. Within one year Zola was promoted three times, ending up as a database manager. This was un-heard of as she was the youngest person in the company. After realizing that she had learned all she could possibly learn, Zola became depressed. "Being a learner, sometimes has its down sides. I realized that I would never be happy at any company, and that I had to do something about it." Because of this Zola started writing the business plan for a mobile spa. Thinking that the spa was too much of a risk, Zola decided to put it aside and try a career change. She never forgot about her spa idea however, and she kept changing and adding to her business plan over the years. After receiving her MBA, Zola became a financial analyst. "The depression set in once again, I became so sad because there was nothing for me to learn, no way for me to grow, and the job responsibilities came with a lot of stress." Zola began to have panic attacks. While sitting at her desk one day, she felt symptoms of what she thought was a heart attack. After going to see a cardiologist, the doctor explained to her that she was actually having anxiety attacks or panic attacks. "I realized that the only time I would have the attacks was at work, as soon as I sat down at my desk. They were uncontrollable." The doctor put her on 30 days leave and told her that she needed to change her life or her career. "While on a leave of absence, I told my husband that I could not go back to work, I felt like I was dying!" "He told me to think about what would make me happy and do it." The next day Zola resigned from her high profile job and salary. Still thinking the spa was too risky, Zola decided to open an Assisted Living Facility. After running the business for a couple of years, the 24/7 care, and her now growing family began to take a toll on her; and once again there was nothing else for her to learn. Operating the Assisted Living Facility taught Zola how to take care of multiple people, how to administer patient bed side care, how to sell and negotiate, and how to thoroughly fill out medical forms and history. These skills would later be used in her own clinic. Zola eventually sold the Assisted Living Facility, but what was she to do now? Feeling like she was at another dead end, Zola began to do some soul searching. What did she really want to do? What job would she be content in, and not want to leave? What would allow her to continuously learn? What did she love to do? Zola pulled out her old business plan and started updating it, and of course went back to school, this time to study skin care. "This is the only field that I could continually learn in. The sky was the limit!"

In 2008, SKYN Clinic & Apothecary was born and open for business. Zola traveled to her client's homes doing Semi-permanent eyelash extensions. She travelled all over the state of Georgia, sometimes up to an hour away from her home; dragging her portable massage table, stool, and her eyelash kit. With her business skills, great customer service, and talents to create and fix things, Zola's business grew fast. "It was hard traveling for work, some of my clients had a lot of stairs, or awkward spaces not conducive for providing good eyelash services. When I became pregnant with my third child, I realized I could not travel around anymore" Zola noted. This led her to start looking for a physical location to provide her services. Zola pulled out the old business plan and started updating it again. This time she expanded her services to provide non-surgical and corrective skin care. "I figured I not only needed to make people look pretty, but I needed to help people. Suffering with adult acne pushed me to research and learn more about non-surgical and corrective skin care".

Determined to provide services that would help people and products that were natural and effective, SKYN Clinic & Apothecary opened in a store front location in the heart of Johns Creek, GA. "All of my services reflect me, they reflect issues that I have had in my life, experiences that I have gone through, and things I have learned. It is my way of helping others correct the skin problems they may have, and build their confidence back up. People just like me." Zola states, "People feel more comfortable when they know you can relate to their concerns, when they know that you have also gone through the same things, and have come through them. Most of all if they can physically see that it has worked for you, then it gives them hope that it will work for them". Zola has done every treatment that she offers in her clinic and has tested every product formulation on herself.

At SKYN Clinic & Apothecary they provide custom blended products. The products are created on the spot and the customer can choose what ingredients they want in their product. Best of all it is free of parabens and harmful substances. SKYN Clinic Custom Blends distributes a vast variety of products for every skin type and condition. One of the most popular products is 'Lash Food'. Lash food is a natural eyelash enhancing serum. It contains no parabens and has less side effects than the other lash growth serums available. It also replenishes needed vitamins to the lash line, and not only causes the eyelashes to grow in length, but also to grow stronger. SKYN Clinic Custom Blends also create products for severe and cystic acne, rosacea, hyperpigmentation, and for anti-aging. Because products are custom blended in the clinic, their potency is 100% stronger than off-the-shelf products.

Zola's eyelash extension work continues to grow. She has completed over 2000 sets of semi-permanent eyelash extensions and has been awarded 'The Best Place for Lashes in Georgia'. She was also one of the first eyelash stylists to learn the internationally acclaimed, Russian Volume technique in the US, and in the state of Georgia. The clinic has also been featured on 'The A-List Atlanta' as one of the best places to go for non-surgical and corrective skin care.

Zola has truly been a visionary, creating the SKYN Clinic & Apothecary brand and becoming a Master Lash Artist, she is a unique combination of business training, talents, leadership skills, discipline, and perseverance. Her advice to beauty professionals, "Never be afraid of change. To live freely, you have to be fearless, and always be a Goal'd Digger!" Now she sees that everything fell into place just perfectly for her to start her own legacy.

"I will admit, I am a Goal'd Digger!"

Contact info:
SKYN Clinic & Apothecary
3630 Peachtree Parkway, Suite 313
Suwanee, GA 30024
Phone: 678.835.8741
FB: Skynclinicapothecary
Twitter: Skynclinic
Pinterest: Skynclinic
IG: Zola_skynclinic
Youtube:skynclinic

Chapter 12

Loreta
JASILIONYTE

Loreta Jasilionyte is the founder of London-based FLAWLESS L'LASHES-European Institute of Master Lash Artists, established in 2013, and accredited and insured with Associated Beauty Therapists.

Loreta also owns and runs the FLAWLESS L'LASHES BEAUTIQUE, which is a successful, busy lash studio in Crawley near Gatwick airport. It was established by Loreta in 2010 after realising a life-long dream of working in the beauty industry. Loreta says about her lash treatments - "Prepare to be WOWED! I will NOT let any of my clients leave my lash studio until their lashes are styled up to the standard that an A-list celebrity would expect!"

After years of enjoying great success in the lash industry, Loreta's passion for styling lashes has grown from strength to strength. She is a London-based Master Lash Stylist who is highly skilled and is in great demand. Her passion for her art is evident in not only the 100% Flawless lash styles that she produces, but also in her dedication to her many eager students who also wish to aspire to become skilled lash artists.

Before getting in to the Beauty business, Loreta was working as a nurse and midwife for four years in neonatal special care, this work taught Loreta to be very responsible, precise and accurate. Even then Loreta's dream was to become a beautician. Whilst nursing, Loreta worked hard to achieve her goal, by attending many different beauty courses back home in Lithuania.

Loreta's beauty background includes working in various beauty salons as a beautician and a nail technician. The most enjoyable treatment for her however, has always been Eyelash Extensions. She has sought to improve this treatment through training with different well known training providers from around the world. Her mission is to raise the standard of eyelash extensions so that each of her students will be confident and highly skilled, and that each of their clients will enjoy a top-class service.

The Flawless L'Lashes Academy has branches in Ireland, Lithuania and the UK offering various training programmes (Foundation, Master, and Russian Volume). All of the branches are run by Master Lash trainers and all of them carry the same outlook when it comes to their work and training etiquette.

Loreta's headquarters and UK base is her home-based salon

and academy in Crawley, London. "My ever supporting husband built me a beauty salon in our back garden to enable me to realise my dream of working in this industry full-time. It is decorated elegantly with a soothing, tranquil atmosphere, where my clients can escape from the hustle and bustle of the outside world while being styled". Eyelash extensions is my passion. I specialise in this field only and my whole entire day is taken up with styling clients, educating students, ordering products for my on-line shop, keeping up to date with my other academy branches (currently in Ireland, Lithuania and the UK), emailing prospective students, supporting current students on my on-line forum, and much much more! I am extremely busy in all aspects of my business and try to set myself apart from others by letting my genuinely helpful and honest personality to shine through when dealing with everyone. It's very easy to become uber-competitive in this industry, but I feel that there is enough business out there for everyone and my motto is to be as helpful as I can to everyone. I hope that everyone finds the success that they are working so hard towards achieving and if I can be even a little part of them achieving their dreams, then it makes all my hard work so worthwhile to me!"

With a growing business and big demand for premium products, Loreta decided to open an internet shop. Flawless L`Lashes luxury brand specialises in the highest quality lash extension products and supplies, designed exclusively for leading international lash stylists.

Their stock is sourced from major manufacturers throughout the world, not restricting them to any particular brand. Their aim is to supply the highest quality products and the most luxurious lashes available, always with an eye on value for money. As manufacturers upgrade and develop new and better products, so Loreta tests and reviews them. Whether it's glue from Germany, tweezers from the USA or lashes from the Far East, her company will only supply the best.

"One of the advantages of working from home is that you're not wasting a couple of hours of the day commuting and travelling. By working from home, I can get people to come to me instead of having to go to them," says Loreta.

Loreta's business tips: if your workload becomes too much and you are not able to spend quality time with your family, then delegate some work to an assistant. Find some quality "you" time - get your own lashes styled, have a soothing back massage. Please ladies - have patience with yourselves and don't be too quick to compare yourself to others who have been styling lashes longer than you - we all had to start somewhere. Once you are methodical and precise in your application, it's only plenty of practice that will get you up to speed. Always up grade your skills, knowledge is Power!

"I love my work. I am inspired by the challenges I face, because they help me improve and discover my full potential. If I do not understand my strengths and my weaknesses, how can I work to improve myself and keep moving ahead?

I love seeing my clients coming back with healthy natural lashes after wearing extensions for years and I love seeing my student's achievements and improvements – they are my inspiration".

Loreta is always trying to find new ways of applying, styling lashes. Recently she was working long days on her own new Volume technique.

"My newest technique for the easiest and slightly fastest way that I can create the perfect lash volume fan."

The Russian colume lash technique is absolutely gripping lash technicians the world over. Most are hungry to perfect this challenging skill than to eat their breakfast!!!

There are a number of ways to create the perfect fan and I have been busy experimenting on my own technique in how to create the perfect fan and place it on the natural lash in a timely manner.

Russian volume styles are exquisite. However, the time it takes to create these works of art is much longer than styling a classical set. I have been tirelessly trying to come up with a technique that shaves some time off the process. My husband has been very patient with me. Most times of late, I am sitting at home deep in practice while he's looking at me forlornly, willing me to give him some attention! it looks like my hard work has paid off as I've put my new technique to practice, with lovely results!

While training and observing students at my academy, E.I.M.L.A. (European Institute of Master Lash Artists), I noticed which steps are the most difficult for most in creating the perfect fans. Hopefully my new technique will make it a bit easier for everybody, like it has done for me.

We are all very lucky these days to have access to a very diverse array of lash extension products, tweezers, etc.

However, after reading everyones' opinions and testimonials on lash forums and groups, I noticed that lash technicians quite often complain that lashes are very hard to peel from the strip or else they are too loose, which is annoying as lashes can be of very good quality but they can make our life more difficult! I came up with this technique which might help to avoid these problems and we can enjoy making fans, without complaining that the product is not right. You are probably thinking how is that possible? It is possible if you are not trying to make a fan before you grab/peel the lashes from the strip.

This technique will be introduced at my academy as a second volume technique. For this technique we use 2 tweezers (a curved one and tweezers which you use for isolating natural lashes, ideal if both have a good grip). The main point is that you are fanning lashes after you peel them from the strip. I will try briefly to explain that in graphic design in a few steps, however there are more details, as to show that in graphic design is practically impossible. It takes only 2-4 seconds, depending how quick a learner you are. I notice that using this technique it is also quite easy to create shorter bases!!

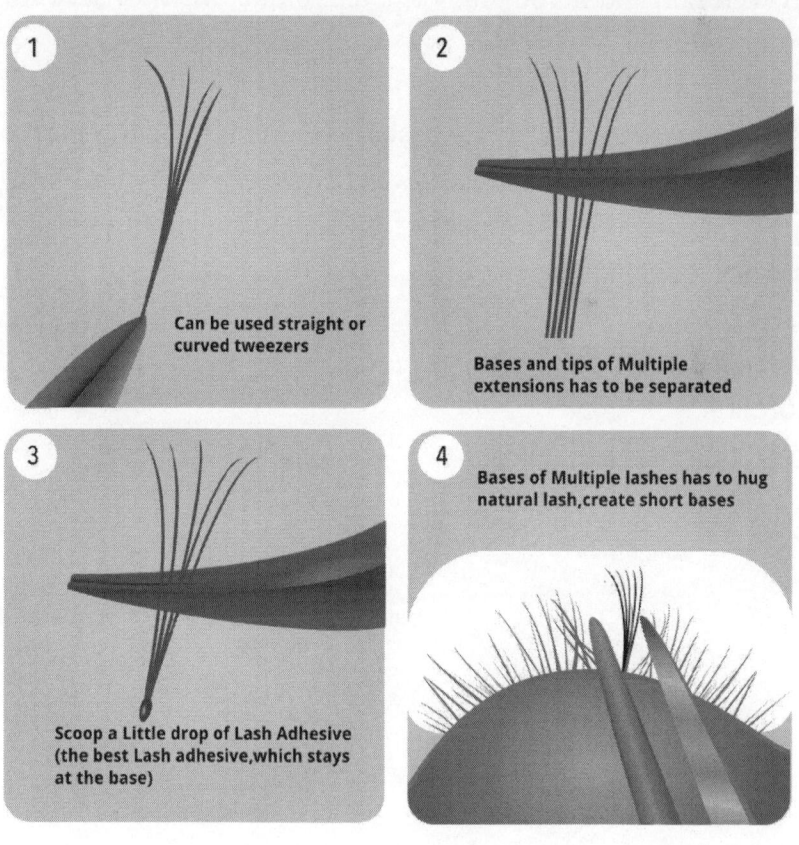

1. Can be used straight or curved tweezers
2. Bases and tips of Multiple extensions has to be separated
3. Scoop a Little drop of Lash Adhesive (the best Lash adhesive, which stays at the base)
4. Bases of Multiple lashes has to hug natural lash, create short bases

Here you can see a sample of graphic design, which shows how it can be achieved. On the course we show you how to achieve this, as tiny details are practically impossible to show in the photos. Using this technique it can speed up a bit of your time creating fans, and you can try different brands of products to achieve the same results. However, it is important to remember that Volume is not about the speed - it is all about the quality, but even if you save an extra few seconds on each fan, and if you enjoy the technique, why not seek for easier options?

I am truly excited at how Russian volume is evolving before our very eyes and will always work tirelessly to try and keep up to date with every aspect of it, hopefully without ending up with a divorce! lol xxx

Sharing Lash Love
Loreta J.
www.eueyelashinstitute.com

Chapter 13

Lindsay **CAREY**

I remember watching my mother get ready in the mornings. She was radiant; dressing in her all-black clothing, transforming simplicity into sophistication. The title 'beauty professional' seems unable to fully illustrate the reach of her work's accomplishments. She possessed her own kind of magic; I watched as, like Cinderella, women changed from cinder-soot to fairy-tale princess, she their fairy Godmother. I knew, with all my heart, my mother was changing the world for those women. I hoped one day I too, could create that kind of change.

Isn't it funny how as children, we never seem to know how small we are? Then, as we grow up, our gaze turns upward and makes us aware of everything bigger than ourselves. I never truly felt small growing up; my mother's sense of limitlessness was infectious - nothing was out of reach, or so it seemed. It wasn't until age 18, after watching my strong, fearless mother battle and eventually be conquered by cancer, I tasted the reality of how small one person can be; for the first time, I feared I was too small for my big dreams.

With her loss barely behind me, I faced choosing my career path; once so clear, I now struggled to know the right decision. I worried the beauty industry would be tainted by my grief; so much of my mother having been connected with the field. However, in visiting aesthetics schools I experienced a welcoming feeling, finding comfort and familiarity, I felt at peace. I've never regretted following my heart, and choosing the beauty industry, nor the decision quickly thereafter: to pursue the strong pull I felt towards lash artistry.

Lash artistry felt like a natural fit. The niche held a two-dimensional fascination for me in its unique mixture of technical precision and artful finesse. Its novelty demanded rigorous refinement of micro-movements, and constant awareness of the latest technical enhancements. My passion spilled over from work; I became mindful of how defining a component the eyes truly are: being an individual's most consistent feature they're key in all communications, highlighting every impression.

Realizing the vast horizon of the lash industry, and riding out the full, exaggerated waves of innovation already happening worldwide, reignited a neglected creative energy, filling me with ideas. Each face became a canvas, the lashes my medium; I realized a woman coming for a lash application trusted me to see and enhance her foundational beauty. My job was accentuating beauty perhaps forgotten, overwhelmed, unappreciated, or simply unused; and each client's reaction felt like an original masterpiece.

Growing as a lash artist cultivated my desire for a professional application tool. Not just any set up, but one that anticipated my every need and held my lashes and adhesive in an ideal way. Even as I tried numerous ways to set up my lashes, I consistently came up short. Frustrated, I began quietly designing my 'Ideal Tool', hoping to stumble across it in one of my fruitless searches. Briefly, the thought occurred to design one myself, but I was quickly overwhelmed by words like CAD designs, prototyping, manufacturing, engineering ...being "just" a beauty professional, I felt so inconsequential. For some time, my ideas stayed inside my notebook, and my mouth stayed shut; I was after all, one small person in a very big world.

In 2013, I attended a Volume Lash training, which was also a catalyst for my product's actualization. The difficulties I - and those training with me- experienced while learning this incredible technique validated the widespread needs my design could potentially meet. The tiny lashes weren't easy to see or pick up; I ached for a lifted palette to hold the lashes closer, easing the strain on my eyes, neck, and back. I wanted a palette to pre-fan the lashes to assist in creating volume fans faster and more efficiently. I imagined the new technique increasing application time, limiting appointments I could take per day - undesirable to myself and my clients. I went home realizing that to increase speed, efficiency and comfort I needed the very product I was creating. Fueled by indignance on behalf of all lash professionals, I continued working on my design - it was time to acknowledge the complexity of lash professionals' capabilities and needs.

Lash artists deserve a set-up system capable of anticipating our kaleidoscope of technical and artistic needs. It must be adaptable enough to allow perfection in each skill level and technique as learned and be as versatile and flexible as the individual utilizing it. We illuminate beauty appreciated by millions; like painters, our tools should be extensions of ourselves, blending in and assisting in creation. Without the need to manage materials throughout application, a lash artist can - like athletes - cease concentrating on individual micro-movements and transcend to a state of continuity, or "flow".

The opportunity to create change for not only myself, but all lash professionals, helped me understand the "magic" I saw my mother perform. I know her differently now; I see her in me, urging me forward when I'm afraid, still teaching me as life moves on. Her "magic" was Karma personified - giving her clients what she cherished most - love, value, confidence. I see the principle repeated in my work, relationships, and the environment: whatever I value, I must first extend. I seek the beauty in all things, and beauty has consistently come back to me, often through others. I've learned it's impossible to be "small" when connected to so many people, in so many ways.

In truth, every big idea was once small; every pro was once an amateur. Growth occurs in the process - be confident that your dreams will become reality. Once I committed to bringing my idea to life, the course began to clear. I made new connections at each step, providing the information necessary to move forward. Overcoming my own self- doubt took longer than the entire production process. So, to others shelving their "big" dreams, believe me when I tell you: There is no such thing as "too small".

A special thank you to Toshi Celaya for helping me tell my story.

Lindsay Carey
Aesthetic Image
www.ailashes.com

Chapter 14

Marisol **PRICE**

"I met so many wonderful women along the years whom are clients and wonderful friends and I want to thank them very much for being such a big part of my lashing journey."

My love for eye lash extensions started when I was enrolled in beauty school in 2005. I was taught in beauty school how to do eyelash "clusters". Unbeknownst to me I was not only the lash prodigy of my class, but in those very moments I was planting the seeds for an amazing future and a passion that I didn't quite know was going to form me into the strong, successful, independent business woman that I am today. I got hit with the lash bug and it just never seemed to leave.

After I graduated from beauty school I did the traditional thing that everyone expected me to do - I cut hair! Men's hair was my focus and love, but I was still never left with that feeling of fulfilment. I have always heard people talking about how they didn't have a career, they had a passion. And as much as I loved cutting hair I never left work with that feeling of "my job is my life, my job is my passion". After some research, soul searching and that lingering lash feeling I had in the back of my mind, I decided to start to lash - or what I thought was lashing, from my home, practicing on my friends and family.

In 2007 I finally had enough confidence and had practiced lashing enough that I did my research, and found a salon that offered a lashing service in Chicago. I set this salon firmly in my sights. This had become my very first in a long series of goals I had set for myself. I booked myself straight in for Xtreme lash training, worked hard, and passed the course. I went to the salon in Chicago; applied for a position, interviewed, and LANDED THE JOB! This was the very first job I had that left the taste of "wanting more" in my mouth. These were the moments when I realized lashing wasn't just work, this wasn't just a job, this was so natural, this was exactly what I meant to do.

I worked at the salon in Chicago and lived in Kenosha WI at the time. During my time working in the city not only did I know lashing was what I was going to do for the rest of my life, but I knew that at the time, the market for this industry in my area was limited and I needed to make it mine. I needed to OWN my lashing market and make my name. I stayed at the salon in Chicago doing lashes for 5 short months and then made a lateral move to the northern suburbs of Illinois.

Over the course of the next 6 years I hit the streets - introducing lashing, its financial potential, and most importantly ME to a series of salons; until my name, my craft, and my genius took off in the form of a raging inferno that left me with no choice but to take the leap of faith. I was terrified. I knew in my mind and in my heart I was amazing at what I did, everyone around me, clients, family and friends alike all encouraged and supported me. They constantly reminded me that this is what I was meant to do. I was left with no choice but to close my eyes take a deep breath as I stepped off the ledge praying to God on my way down that I was making the right decision – to finally bring Ooh'lah Lash to life.

It is currently 2014. As I stand here staring at myself in the mirror, the pillar of the industry that I am today, I need to thank you all. I need to thank the salons that told me no! I need to thank the professionals that told me lashing was never going to go anywhere! If it was not for people like you that kept knocking me down, I would never have had the fire to become who I am. On the flip side of life: to my family, friends and clients - I would not be where I am without you. You picked me up when I fell, you encouraged me when I felt lost, you pushed me when I needed to be pushed, and you loved me when you all knew I needed to be loved just that little bit more. If it were not for you, all the good, the bad and the ugly; I would not be able to sit here today and tell you my story. I would not be able to tell, teach, and encourage other women to embrace who they are. Embrace your passion. Own your craft. Take the leap. Trust yourself. Work your ass off and live! Loving what you do in life is the best kind of living you can have.

My future is a mystery to me. I will never stop setting goals for myself. I will never stop creating my own empire. I will continue to grow Ooh'lah Lash and myself. I hope someday to educate, brand and expand.

If I could offer any advice to any up and coming lash artists it would be this: Always be in the know, never stop educating yourself, practice and patience some more, these things will help make you a great lash artist.

I have met so many wonderful women along the years, both clients and friends, and I would like to thank them very much for being such a huge part of my lashing journey.

Finally, I would like to dedicate my story to my late brother Juan. He suddenly passed away in 2013 and was one of the biggest supporters of my journey.

Ooh'lah Lash
1788 Second Street
Highland Park, Il 60035
www.oohlahlash.com
847-751-5274

Chapter 15

Ria (Sotiria) **HOUNTAS**

Hi! I'm Ria Hountas, I've been a professional Lash Artist since 2007 and am the founder of LASHTIQUE in New York. It's truly an honor to be amongst this amazing group of talented and professional women. It's also quite an honor that YOU are reading this and I thank you.

I always knew I wanted to help people. I am as passionate about medicine, health and wellness as I am about beauty and its relationship to the person as a whole. My first job in high school was in a dermatology office. I was obsessed with learning about skin, about different conditions and how to make it better. There was a small component of cosmetic dermatology as well. Naturally that was also a major interest. I worked there for a few years through my early days of college in which I did the 'tour de schools'. I started at a community college, then transferred to a city college which lasted all of a week. I was always a bit of a dreamer. I wanted to create something for myself while helping people. Coming from parents who had immigrated here from Greece, I would hear nothing else from them than for me to finish school. I could do whatever I wanted after but needed to finish that degree. At one point I was considering medical school but I knew myself, I knew I needed a different type of flexibility and the school commitment rather frightened me. Exploring further I considered becoming a physician's assistant and ultimately decided to become a registered nurse. Nursing appealed to me in sooooo many ways, it had so many niches and specialities. However while my mother would have liked me to make a lifelong career working the ranks in a hospital setting, I had already began discovering that I didn't have an interest in that. I enjoyed the flexibility of a schedule and also all the different types of nursing I could do. I knew that I (and my self-diagnosed ADD) needed to feel that I have options. Whatever I focused on I gave 110% but the security I sought was that if I wanted to make a change, I could. The other component of nursing that drew me in was the nursing philosophy and the integrated approach of health and wellness. The "whole-istic" approach that an alteration in one system affects the whole.

My decision was made, I enrolled in a nursing program and 3.5 years later I obtained a Bachelor of Science degree in Nursing. My first job was a pediatric hematology oncology nurse at the prestigious Sloan Kettering Cancer Center in NYC. A truly humbling experience that I consider myself so fortunate to have had. As difficult as it was, it grounded me. I learned so much about inner strength. These children, the families and the dynamics changed my perspective on life and knew that I would carry that forward for the rest of my life. I knew that I wouldn't be working there forever but my career there was short lived following a severe back injury. I was devastated and actually fell into a very deep depression. I worked so hard to be where I was and felt I wasn't done with that component of my career yet. After about a year of rehab, I began working for an allergy and immunology practice. It was good to get back to working, I always enjoyed learning something new but it was difficult being in constant pain since it still was a physically demanding position. During this time I was contemplating going to go back to school to do further masters study and obtain a nurse practitioner degree.

The day then came that changed my life, while I didn't know it yet, life was preparing to take me down a totally different path. So there I was, on the couch, in my living room, flipping through the pages of Vogue when an article caught my eye. It was about eyelash extensions. My initial reaction was rather volatile (which caught me by surprise since I'm usually rather mellow), my heart started racing, I can feel my blood pressure rising and I actually spoke to myself aloud: "Really?! Now our eyelashes aren't good enough as is?!?!?" "Great, something else we need to maintain" and "This is BS!" I closed the magazine and tossed it onto the coffee table. Sitting there, stunned with my reaction, I reflected for a while. It wasn't too long before I calmed down, looked over to the magazine on the table and did that exaggerated slow reach back to grab the magazine so

I could examine its contents a little further. Let's just say that it probably took me only a few minutes to get up, go into my office and begin my frantic internet searches of where I could go and have this done. Not only did I need to have it done, I needed it NOW.

I couldn't afford to go to the pro listed in Vogue and there weren't many around at the time. Only 2 in the city. I started asking around and found a place in Chinatown. Off to the city I went. I wasn't sure what to expect. Laying there I was like "Am I really doing this?" Yup. I did it. I had about 20 extensions on each eye (that used to be the average for a full set those days) and looking in the mirror I said "WOW". Ok, I get it, I sooooo get why this was article worthy. I paid my $400 dollars and had a little pep in my step walking out. I'll admit, I was a little nervous. The place I went to wasn't exactly the most hygienic. As an RN and totally germ phobic this irked me but I caught another glance in the mirror and I was quickly back to "wow" thoughts.

I went on my merry way, calling my girlfriends etc. I was completely taken with the subtle enhancement that had such a profound effect on my appearance without any makeup. I haven't felt comfortable being out and about without any makeup since I was a kid!

Fast forward a few months and one of my best girlfriends Oksana, who is a professional make-up artist specializing in bridal, brought up the lashes again saying how brides are starting to ask for them. She mentioned to me casually one day that perhaps I should look into providing the service.. I was like, I really think I can do it but I wanted to get back to school until I realized it might be worth investigating a little further. And I did, oh I did. I found everything that existed on the internet about the service. I thought to myself, wow, this could be a great way to go back to school and have the flexibility to go to school without having to worry about what my employer would say with changes to my schedule every semester with the intense nursing program and clinical sessions. I did my research and decided to train with Xtreme Lashes. I liked the fact that the company was founded by an RN as well. I told myself that I will give this a chance, if I find that I do not have the skills I will let it go but I felt okay to take that step.

I signed up for a private class instead of a group course. I figured it would be a bit more immersive. Well my private class which was to be a min of 6 hours was somehow only 3. We read the manual together and I got to apply a whole 4 lashes per eye to my friend who was to be my practice model, before I was sent on my way with a pat on the back. I was a bit disappointed with the initial teaching but I knew I was resourceful. The company offered me an opportunity to sit in on another class free of charge. It was difficult. It meant another day off work and inconveniencing a friend again to take time off work to be a practice model. Fortunately I had found a forum online with other lash pro's and we all found encouragement together. I practiced and practiced and practiced some more. The adhesives were very slow drying at the time so the process was very very slow.

While I was practicing I made a few decisions about how I wanted to proceed. I knew nothing of starting a business other than knowing I wanted to. What I did know was that I wouldn't put myself out there until I had confidence in my abilities, in being able to have my clients trust my abilities, and that I could provide them with proper service. I also knew that I wanted to enter at a certain price point and not start by offering discounted services.

I practiced on everyone that would let me. I made sure to have variety of ages, lash types and shapes. I made sure that I practiced on my "models" through not one but a few touch ups, so I knew what to expect and understood the behaviours of the natural lashes with the extensions, I knew the durability and also my models feedback. I explored a variety of styling options on the same eyes so I could understand the aesthetic range I could create. What would be flattering and what wouldn't be. This process lasted a few months. I was fortunate that I didn't struggle with the actual application technique. Do not misunderstand this and think for a moment there weren't times I wanted to throw my tweezers to the wall and give up. There were plenty of those but my slightly OCD tendencies wouldn't allow that. I had to be able to "get it". I believe that is a trait most lash artists share. Can you relate?

LASH MASTERS

A lash mentor, Jill, once told me that starting a business is like planting your own garden. You take a seedling and you nurture it, tend to it and watch it grow. That is etched in my mind forever. I had some wonderful support and also had some people close to me that were not so supportive. I realized that it was their own fears projected and I can in no way allow that to affect me. And I didn't. When I finally launched LASHTIQUE in 2007 I felt ready to enter the world as a lash artist. The nervous excitement was rather exhilarating. I was finally creating something of my own. At 30 years old I finally felt I was listening to my calling. At this point I still had every intention of going back to grad school. I didn't know that this would become what it did. I knew that it was a stepping stone. I thought it would be a part time thing and even though I intended for it to be a means to get through school, I still took it seriously. If I was going to do it, I was going to do it right, be it for a client base of a few or of many.

I remember my first paying client at my full intended prices. I was nervous but kept telling myself I was ready and I would just have to do it. I thought I had it together and everything was totally under control. She was a bride and getting married in a week. Yep, extra pressure. I kept telling myself "I got this". I felt ok, I was about to begin, and my hands just Wouldn't. Stop. Shaking. Now that made me nervous, sharp pointy tweezers, a procedure that requires surgical precision, and there I am with uncontrollable shaking hands. I had to get a grip and quick, it was almost comical. I was hoping that she couldn't feel my shaking hands on her forehead. It took about 10 minutes and with some breathing I got into my flow. Two and a half hours later I was done. I was eager to see her reaction and found comfort when she was ecstatic. It was instant comfort and a serious confidence boost. When she had left, I couldn't believe that it went so well considering the ummm, shaky start! I couldn't believe that in two and a half hours I made more than I would all day as a nurse, and I couldn't believe that she was thrilled! I couldn't believe that was the feeling after taking that first step.

After that, with each client and each referral I no longer had the same nerves. No more shaky hand syndrome. Always excited when I would get a new message and more calls coming in. My confidence, my speed and my passion was flourishing. Not only that but I LOVED providing this service. It was soothing, it was like meditation and I was just as addicted as my clients.

Within 6 months it was time to make a decision. I was working 35 hours a week as an RN, I was seeing about 6 steady clients per week and it was getting more difficult to manage both and really, all I wanted to do was lash all day every day. I was apprehensive because I also needed a steady income. Was it time to quit my nursing job and focus just on lashes and take the leap of faith? I did and am so happy. They always say the first step is the hardest. It really is. Once I became more available even more and more phone calls came in. I was thrilled. When I wasn't seeing clients I was practicing and "playing" with different looks and ways I could improve my speed and efficiency. I was reading on how to run a business and working out what my next step should be. I started doing mobile services at client's homes. After a while when I was getting busier I knew I needed to have a location. I feel that it's important to know yourself and know the environment you want to work in. I knew that I didn't want to work in a salon environment. It was such a soothing service I didn't want the buzz to interrupt that flow. I sought out daily room rentals that were non spa or salon spaces. I looked for acupuncture and massage spaces. It worked out well, I was able to find places I could book a few hours or pay a day rate and didn't have to commit to a monthly rent. I was able to establish myself slowly and it gave me time to feel secure in some steady income before making a longer term commitment. I kept on searching for spaces and ultimately went into a shared space arrangement for 4 days a week. It was perfect. I always knew that if I had to, I could go into a spa and work out a commission arrangement. I was fortunate, I didn't need to.

I loved going to work every day and knew that I was changing lives with a subtle enhancement. My client base was quite diverse and very empowering. I had doctors and lawyers and entrepreneurs and students and socialites and stay at home moms and high level executives of fortune 500 companies and eventually my client list included some celebrities. I had clients who hardly ever wore make up to clients who seemed to roll out of bed glamorous. Younger women, older women, every socioeconomic background. A dynamic range of personalities. I was giving them confidence, and it was so much more than that. I provided them with increased confidence while wearing less makeup. It was so powerful and their reactions fueled my passion even more. Women can't get enough of them, I can't get enough of giving them. They quickly become something you can't live without. All my clients repeatedly state how this service is the most important beauty treatment they have.

I've enjoyed having my business as a solo lash artist. I believe not being in a storefront environment and keeping it a secret service gave me a competitive edge. My clients loved that we would have our sessions in a quiet, nurturing environment that truly provided an escape for them. Their feedback reinforced that I was making the right decisions. Often they mentioned to me that they were pleased that they didn't have to go to a salon environment for this type of service. I was glad to hear that because it matched my personality more. I was attracting the right type of clients for me. It makes a big difference.

There is an interesting and profound energy exchange with this service. I do more than provide a great set of lashes for my clients. There is a big "therapist" component to the service. Another thing I learned was that many clients aren't simply seeking the service. They are seeking the experience as well.

What is the experience you would like your clients to have?

Another part that I felt distinguished me was that I was really able to tune into what the client wanted. I was able to adapt their style to their lifestyle. I took the time to communicate with them and tailor my style to them. I used many different sizes in my sets and the way that I blended them. Much more than the few sizes that I was taught. My clients would repeatedly inform me how no one knew they had extensions and they even fooled people in the industry. Word spreads quickly, I have to say.

The other point I need to make is the power of intention. I remember driving home one day after a few clients and asking myself how people get into magazines or publicity. I remember saying to myself- "that would be great, I would love that". I was exhausted so I didn't search the internet for answers. The next afternoon I receive a voicemail from a CBS 2 news producer that wanted to do a feature on lashes. I called back right away and set everything up for a few days later. Seriously- how uncanny is that?! All went well except my shaky hand syndrome returned violently as soon as the camera went on. I had to pause the taping. How could they film me with sharp tweezers and shaky hands?? I was able to get a grip and it went very well. The journalist was amazed and booked an appointment with me on the spot. That provided me with a huge new client boost. I was fortunate to have a few more really great publicity pieces that just happened to come my way. I was amazed and again, humbled. I'd only been in the industry a year. This all confirmed that I was making the right decisions. Baby steps but baby steps in the right direction. After CBS I was fortunate to have other media opportunities and my reach began to expand further.

If you are reading this and starting out in the industry I would advise you to visualize how you would like your business to be. Take steps that support that visualization. Network with other professionals and entrepreneurs even in other fields. You will be amazed at the energy exchanges and the recourses they could provide. The next thing I would say is take your time to make sure you are armed with as much knowledge as you can possibly be. Don't rush the process of this learning. Once you have a solid foundation, progress can happen in leaps and bounds. I knew I wanted to be at the higher price points of this service. I took steps to ensure that, and it was working in my favour. Look within yourself and see which direction you would like to go in. Just do not undervalue what you are worth. Do not allow your fears to hinder you. While it's always good to have a comparative of others as far as what you like and what you don't like, do not be intimidated nor feel that you have to be priced under. You are you and your clients will want to come to you for all that you provide for them and have great lashes as a bonus.

The most important tip I can offer in this short chapter is the importance of consistency. You cannot allow whatever else may be going on in your life to interfere with your service. Or other distractions for that matter. When your client is lying there with you, be 100% present and focused on them and the art of lashes. If a client feels that they are getting a steady, constant level of service, they will for the most part remain loyal to you. Consistency is one of my biggest things. Think of when you found a great restaurant, you went a few times and it was always great, service and quality of food was always on point and then you go back and it wasn't. Perhaps you went again forgiving it as a one off time and found yourself disappointed again. That's not a good feeling right? How about a hair dresser or another beauty service, the first few times were great and then you noticed a decline once they got more comfortable with you. It makes you want to start looking for someone who can make you look and feel great again doesn't it? Don't be that person that just gets too comfortable. Try and exceed their expectation each and every time. The power of lashes is a great one, something special happens that is difficult to compare to any other service. You are the person who holds that power, for yourself, as a practitioner and for your client. Embrace it and the process.

Thank you for reading my chapter. I truly hope at least one thing resonated for you. I wish you great success and always feel free to reach out and connect.

http://www.lashtique.com
http://www.shbeauty.com
718-974.2821
ria@lashtique.com

Final Words of Wisdom

Fodoulla Nicolaou

After qualifying with a level 2 NVQ in Beauty Therapy at Stafford College, I went to Manchester and trained with Lash Perfect in 2008. I loved the course, and I knew from that moment, lashes were going to be MY thing! From then onwards, all I have done is lash extensions, nothing to do with my NVQ! I have a big client base coming from Birmingham, Stoke and many of the surrounding towns, just from word of mouth recommendations! I have only just recently added a few other exclusive treatments as I wanted people to know me for my passion for 'Luscious Lashes'. My advice would be, find a good company who care about how they teach, and practice practice practice ... and really love what you are doing for people - that will make them love and appreciate your service for years to come. I have had loyal clients with me from day one. I love lashing , it was the best decision I made in taking that course.

http://www.luscious-lashes-stafford.co.uk/

Lucy Argent

I have been doing eyelash extensions now for over 10 years. As the only job I have ever had, lashes have become my life. Three years ago I opened the first lash bar in Cambridge, it has gone from strength to strength with every year we have been open. After training with AH Francis in 2004, I was one of a handful of lash technicians in the UK. Travelling up and down the country doing eyelashes, I soon became a trainer. I have now been training for over 5 years spreading the lash love. Being apart of this industry for so long I enjoy training others as well as always learning myself. In 2008 I was offered to set up and run the first 5* spa in Mongolia. The hotel and spa was part of Small Hotels of the World. Taking eyelash extensions to Outer Mongolia was a huge success. It was something the country had never seen before, but certainly something that is going to stay. Back in the UK I trained in the New Russian volume technique with Irina Levchuk and it is definitely the next generation of lashes ... I can't wait to see what's next!

http://www.thesalonatno5.co.uk/

Printed in Great Britain
by Amazon.co.uk, Ltd.,
Marston Gate.